Welcome to Walla Walla

Sam McLeod

To Annie
From Sam

The Beginning

April 2005

Hi. My name is Sam. Well, it's not really Sam; Sam is my pen name. I'm not trying to hide anything; I just always wanted to have a pen name and I've always liked the name, Sam McLeod.

Before I get too far, you should know that I grew up in the South. I talk a little "slow." So I'm suggesting you read this book "slow." If you don't, it'll seem juvenile. It might seem juvenile anyway.

This book is dedicated to Annie. Annie is my wonderful wife of 30 years. (I'm going to get a lot of points for saying that on paper.) Actually, her name's not really Annie. She said that if I had a pen name, she wanted a new name, too. She likes to keep things even.

On our 29th wedding anniversary, Annie said she wanted me to write a book and give it to her for our 30th anniversary. I think she was really saying that I'd been talking about writing a book for a long time and needed to get on with it. Well, here it is. This is the best I could do on short notice.

I also wrote this book for our three terrific daughters—Summer, Jolie, and Marshall. These are not their

1

real names either. They didn't care too much about keeping things even, but they liked the idea of being able to choose names different from the ones we gave them.

In March 2004 Annie and I decided to go off on an adventure and moved from Seattle to Walla Walla. This book is about our new life. I've always heard that folks should write from experience, and our move has been an experience—mostly a good one.

This book is also dedicated to friends, family and the Walla Wallans who provided bits and pieces of the characters in this book. All of the characters are part real and part fabricated. So are the stories. I like this quote:

> . . . Someone once defined fiction as just something a writer made up and nonfiction as just something a writer made up using the names of real people . . . I've given this some thought, and I think my standard recollection . . . is made up of the emotion of the moment, the mood of the day, the scenery, the company, the weather, who I am, who I think I am, who I'd like to be, my own sense of poetry, and a few tattered shreds of what actually happened.
>
> *At the Grave of the Unknown Fisherman*
> by John Gierach

I think that quote describes pretty well how the stories in this book came to be.

So, if you are a friend, or family member, or a Walla Wallan and read this book and think that a certain character is you or may be you, I can tell you now that you're mostly wrong.

If you are a friend, or a family member, or a Walla Wallan and are easily offended and think that everything's always about you, just don't read the book. That'll save us both some heartache.

If you don't find a character that you think is you or probably you but you wish there were one, then let me know. If you are an interesting person and would like to get in a book, I'd like to get to know you so I'll have something interesting to write about if I ever write another one.

As I said, Annie and I decided to move to Walla Walla about a year ago. Folks are always asking us, "Why Walla Walla?" Maybe this book will help explain why . . . or maybe not. I don't know. You'll have to decide for yourself.

Sam

Get a Life

Christmas came on slow and ended real quick in a confusion of duffle-toting exits. The house had filled to overflowing with kids, friends, and relatives just long enough for everybody to eat too much, drink too much and open too many presents. The holiday party was a short one; if I said 48 hours, I'd be stretching it.

Leftovers from Christmas dinner filled the icebox. There was a tired-looking turkey carcass half covered in foil sitting on a huge platter surrounded by dry crusty dressing and wilted parsley. And there were green beans in a disposable plastic bowl with a blue top, cranberry sauce in a glass bowl covered in pink plastic wrap, and bread pudding overflowing a baking dish. Empty wine bottles waited their turn in the recycling bin. Holiday china was stacked on the kitchen counter to go back on the top shelf of the pantry whenever Annie or I could muster the energy to haul out the stepladder.

Nobody could figure out how I'd managed to fix bread pudding with the consistency of water-soaked cardboard, but I'd done it, and the full baking dish shoved toward the back of the refrigerator told the story. "Wow, that was a great dinner, Dad," they said. "We're just too stuffed to eat dessert," they said. "Save it Dad; we'll have some later," they said. "But this is really good Dad," they said. "Maybe you could make it again some day, Dad." Well, at least they were polite about it.

Empty boxes, crumpled wrapping paper and shredded ribbon filled up the garbage. Red sweaters, flannel pajamas, new books still in their jacket covers, skimpy underwear, various electronic gadgets, bracelets, earring boxes and opened Christmas cards lay scattered in messy piles all over the house. Stained napkins were still wrapped around half-empty pop cans and wine glasses. "We'll put it away," they said. "We'll take this stuff back with us the next time we're here," they said. "Gotta run," they said.

Our two older daughters, Summer and Jolie, had been home for all of a few hours and gone again. Summer, our oldest and a recent college graduate, had red-eyed her way back to her job and boyfriend in Virginia. Jolie, our middle child, was off on a short skiing trip with friends before returning to college in Walla Walla for the last semester of her junior year. Our youngest daughter, Marshall, was still living at home but, just five months shy of high school graduation, spent most of her time at school, training her horse or hanging out with friends. She'd breeze through the house occasionally to change clothes and rifle through the kitchen cupboards, but was not otherwise around much anymore. Annie's mom was back in Virginia with the rest of Annie's family. My mom and brother had just called to say that they were back in Nashville where my family is still centered. The house was all the sudden a real quiet place.

Annie and I sat in front of a roaring fire on the sun porch staring empty-eyed at the flames. Babe, the dog, slept on the rug in front of the fire. Frank Sinatra sang holiday songs for the umpteenth time in the background. The post-holiday blues were setting in. "We need to get a life," Annie said.

* * * * * * * * * *

As I told you before, my name is Sam. I grew up in Nashville—a combination of Southern gentleman and Johnny Cash. Back in 1969, I went north to college at the University of Virginia—"Mr. Jefferson's University" we call it.

I survived Woodstock, the spring of '70 and Kent State, the Grateful Dead and four years of an all-male school punctuated by alcohol-laced trips to women's colleges in the vicinity of Charlottesville. I had a great time and, given half a chance, would go back and do it all over again.

I met Annie in Charlottesville on an ill-fated blind date set up by Annie's friend Mary Minor. Unfortunately, I'd developed a bad cold earlier in the day. We sat in front of a TV watching a football game that neither of us cared about, half-heartedly drinking beer, and wishing that we were somewhere else—with somebody else. A few weeks later I called Annie up and said, "I can do better; give me another shot." And that started it.

Annie had grown up in Virginia. She was blonde-haired, blue-eyed, perky and full of words stretched out by a southern accent that parodies are made of. When I met her, she was studying to be a speech therapist. Occasionally she'd take me to visit with her patients, many of whom were developing noticeable southern drawls. Over time, and overcoming a little lumpiness in the relationship, we fell in love and got married.

So, here's the short version of a longer story: Annie supported me through graduate school. She drew the line there and said I should look for a new wife if I wanted to keep on avoiding getting a job. I've been a banker, a lawyer and an investor. Annie has been a speech therapist, the mother of three great daughters, and a charity volunteer at a bunch of places. We've lived in six cities over thirty years of marriage. Our kids have taken ballet lessons (largely ineffective); played soccer, basketball, lacrosse, volleyball, and softball; run cross-country and ridden horses. They've done well in school (most of the time), gone to college and had more friends and boyfriends than I can count or remember. We've spent a lot of quality family time talking about and worrying over hair and boyfriends. Our daughters have turned out great—mostly Annie's doing.

The stock market was good to us. We bought the Seattle house with the lake views, acquired lots of stuff, remodeled and fixed up, and entertained. I sold my business and retired about a year ago—earlier than I'd expected.

We'd lived the life we were "supposed" to live and, with occasional detours along the way, had pretty much done it right. "Been there, done that," Annie says. Unfortunately, we were bored with the storybook life that we always thought would make us happy.

As we sat in front of that roaring fire, we realized that we were pretty much waiting for the kids to get married and produce a bunch of grandkids we could spoil for a while before we died.

Now *I* said it, "We need to get a life."

* * * * * * * * * *

What is a life anyway? (We didn't know and probably still don't.) Hang around Seattle, pick up some volunteer jobs, help humanity, wait for the kids to come home, and then wait for the kids to have kids and come home? Move to a Caribbean island, fish all day, have a drink and watch the tide roll out in the evenings? Join the Peace Corps? Move to wine country and start a winery? Do some teaching somewhere? Move "home" to Nashville or Richmond and hang out with the family? Or something else? There were lots of possibilities but pitifully little guidance.

Annie said we should make a list of things we liked to do and things we'd always wanted to do but hadn't done. And I said we needed a list of places that'd always attracted us—places we'd been and wanted to see again or places we'd always wanted to go visit. And Annie said let's make a list of friends and family that are important to us, and how they could figure in. We both agreed, a new life had to be an adventure—something that got your heart pumping. So, we did. We made separate lists, then combined lists, then culled lists, and on and on until we had a picture of the future we both wanted and were excited about.

The lists boiled themselves down to friends and family, a small friendly town, a simpler life with less stuff cluttering the place up, wide open spaces, animals, outdoor activities like fishing and hiking, a place where we could learn new things, and with the good hospitals and doctors that we'd need in our dotage.

* * * * * * * * * *

So, we looked all over, talked to a bunch of folks and settled on Walla Walla, Washington as our new home. Everybody (and I mean *everybody*) said, "Why Walla Walla?" And we gave back too-long answers about a small town that hadn't been discovered yet where there were nice people living quieter lives uncluttered with big city obstacles, where there were young people at local colleges keeping the place lively, where we could afford to buy some land and build a house and a barn out in the country, where the sun shines a lot, where we could have a few dogs and other animals, where I could hunt and fish, where there was a lot to do with wineries, local college events and local town events, and where you could sit on the porch in the evening and watch the ducks and geese passing through while a big roaring fire warmed your feet.

There were lots of reasons to move to Walla Walla but the real one was "because we wanted to." Even though that didn't satisfy everybody else, it satisfied us. And if you're going to get a life, maybe it's better to get the one you want than the one somebody else wants you to have.

* * * * * * * * * *

We went looking for a piece of land near Walla Walla—a place where we could base our new life. Unless you are bedridden and have been watching TV soap operas all day, every day for a few months, you really wouldn't be much interested in the details. I think it is probably enough to say that over a few months of talking to folks around town and to their friends and friends of friends, we found a piece of pasture land out in the Walla Walla Valley right on the Walla Walla River just a stone's throw (a long one) from several local wineries, and 15 minutes from the center of town. The views are big—the Blue Mountains to the east, the Horse Heaven Hills with their windmills to our south, big views down valley to the Pasco Basin to our west, and the edge of the rolling Palouse Hills to our north. We were taken with the beautiful dawns, pink sunsets, and open sky filled with stars at night. Annie said it felt right to her and, while I don't have her sensitivity to the mystical, I had to agree, it felt right. We called it "The Land" (because, at the time, we didn't have a better name). Within weeks we were moving to Walla Walla.

I guess I should apologize for what comes next. Over the year following our discovery of The Land, I wrote a truckload of letters to friends and family who inquired about this or that along the way. I also kept a journal for the first time in my life. It was all new to us—Walla Walla, The Land, farming, keeping animals, water rights, wildlife habitat, noxious weeds and drought-resistant grasses, wind, town folk and country folk, festivals, rodeos, parades, wineries, art galleries, local college sports, and on and on. We had a lot to learn and we learned a lot. Whether it was the right stuff, we still don't know; but, right or wrong, we learned it and I regularly bored our friends and family with my findings. I figured it was okay if I was wrong in what I was reporting. If I didn't know what was true and what wasn't, how would they? So, I passed it on. Here are some of the letters I sent them . . . I hope you're not one of those folks who believes everything you read.

Sam

Moving to
Walla Walla

April 2004

Dear Bert,

Sorry it's been such a long time since I've written. I hope that this letter finds you well and that you'll write me back so we can get reconnected. Annie is on me to develop some friends. She thinks I need more connections in my life and she thinks I need some other people to do stuff with so I won't be bugging her all the time. I guess she's right. Anyway, I'm going to give it a shot. With any luck, Margie is on you about the same stuff, so maybe we can help each other out.

The girls are thriving. Summer graduated from the University of Virginia and found a job in Charlottesville at the children's museum teaching little kids about the universe. So, good for her; I guess studying anthropology at college worked out okay after all.

I didn't know she knew anything about the universe, but she must if they're letting her teach it. She goes to elementary schools with a blowup universe that you can sit inside of with all the kids. She doesn't think I'd last a minute inside this thing with all those kids screaming and bouncing around in it. But she likes it.

Jolie is still in college. She goes to Whitman College over in Walla Walla, which is a small farming town in Washington State way over in the southeast corner of the state right next to Oregon and Idaho. She loves Whitman and Walla Walla, and is studying politics as a major so she can be a nursery school teacher. I guess that makes as much sense as studying anthropology so you can teach about the universe.

Jolie says she wants to reform the educational system and teach nursery school when she graduates. Seems like an awful lot to bite off but if anybody can do it she can. She's the busiest thing you've ever seen. Annie and I go over to visit her sometimes and it's hard to get on her calendar. So that leaves us with a lot of time on our hands to wander around Walla Walla on our own and that's how we've come to know it and fall in love with the place. We'll be moving over there this coming fall. I'll write you more about that another time.

Marshall is going off to college in September at Central Washington University in Ellensburg. She wants to work with animals and communicate with them using sign language. CWU has a great program doing just that. Marshall's our only daughter who wants to study something in college and then use it. She is our animal girl and will almost surely find a way to turn her love for animals into a job one of these days.

Marshall has been riding horses forever and is good at it. She's really happy about our move to Walla Walla because we'll be pretty close to Ellensburg and maybe she can come over to Walla Walla and ride some. I've told her that we're not having any animals on our farm that are bigger than we are, but I think she thinks I'll give in and let her keep a horse over there. I won't, but that's a battle I don't have to fight today.

So there's an update on the kids. No husbands or grandchildren yet, but we're hoping they'll get on with it when the time is right. Annie is ready to be a grandma whenever it happens, but I keep telling her we don't need to be in any rush. It'll happen soon enough and we don't have anything to say about it anyhow.

I think you know that I sold my business about a year ago and ended up retired sooner than I had planned. All I've ever done is work, so I don't really have any hobbies to fill up my time. I've been thinking on what to do next for a while now and hadn't really come up with any brilliant ideas until Annie suggested a small farm as a project for me—a little weekend place for us to go to. We started planning it in our heads and slowly realized that there's no way to do a part-time farm with animals and a garden and other stuff. You have to do it full time. So, that's when we settled on the idea of moving to Walla Walla and setting up a farm of our own.

Annie and I finally figured out that sitting around Seattle waiting for the children and grandchildren to show up was going to be a lot of waiting and not much doing, and that we're not dead yet and are up for another adventure. So we're just going to go do it. People ask us all the time if we know what we're doing. The answer is no; we don't. And thank goodness. In my experience, adventures aren't much fun if you know what's going to happen.

We'll keep you posted on our progress. And please write me back and tell me what you and Margie and your boys are doing so I can show Annie that I'm connecting up with other human beings and keeping myself busy.

Best,
Sam

The Land

April 2004

Dear Larry:

Thank you for your letter. We're glad that you're so enthusiastic about our upcoming move. We are putting you number one on our list of folks to invite out to visit when our new house gets built. I think I told you that we are moving to Walla Walla in late August and are planning to rent a little house downtown until the new house is ready for us. Annie thinks we'll get into the new place before the end of the year, and she has got Greg, our builder, nodding his head like he agrees with her; but I'm betting on some time early next year. Anyway, we'd love to have you guys come visit when the new place gets built.

Ever since we bought our property, we've referred to it as "The Land." It doesn't have an address yet (although we have applied to the local county officials for one). The old country road we're on is Detour Road—a good name from the perspective of a couple taking a big detour off the road of a predictable life. This detour is either another one of our hair-brained schemes or an adventure worthy of our next life, depending on your perspective—and you are welcome to your perspective. Everybody else we know seems to have one, and we haven't paid much attention to theirs either.

Detour Road was probably a real detour road at some point in the past so road crews could work on the main highway. We'll have to check into the road work history, but investigating this bit of The Land's background has not made its way onto our near-term "to do" list. At some point, maybe we'll give The Land another name; something original like "Detour Farm." And maybe we'll get creative and work up a little logo for Detour Farm so we can do T-shirts and baseball caps. If we do, I'll send you and Sharon a couple of shirts.

The Land is 160 acres "more or less"—according to the deed. At this point, it's pasture-land of tall wheatgrass and longhorn fescue and all manner of weeds with about a hundred head of red angus cattle grazing it—mostly cows and their calves, but with a couple of huge bulls thrown in just to keep us new and timid farmers a little off balance. I've seen enough TV shows

on bullfighting to convince me that being trampled by a bull is not a pleasant way to spend a day. And I'll admit that I'm even a little uncomfortable if one of the big heifers gets too curious about whatever I happen to be doing out in her pasture.

We are bordered on the east by three farms raising alfalfa, wheat, cattle, and probably some crops and animals that we haven't seen or identified yet. We're bordered on the west by a big alfalfa field that will sure smell good when the alfalfa blooms in the spring. Detour Road is our southern border and the Walla Walla River sets our northern border. The river is a little unpredictable; it's a trickle in the dead of summer when folks are irrigating their farms, and it rages in late winter when the snow melts in the Blue Mountains and early spring rains start to fall. In between, it's anybody's guess what she'll be doing.

The "160 acres more or less" wording in the deed is a function of two things. First, almost none of the land around us has ever been surveyed. Over time, fence lines have set boundaries mostly to keep animals in or out (depending on which side of the fence you're on). As a practical matter, whatever the deed may say, these fence lines are so well accepted by the neighbors that no piece of paper is likely to convince anybody that property boundaries are anything different from what they can see looking out the kitchen window.

Second, the north border of The Land is set by the changing pattern of the Walla Walla River as it meanders through the valley. Our property line on the north extends to the middle of the river wherever that may be at any point in time. Big spring rains and snowmelt out of the Blue Mountains to the east of us combined to fill up the river back in March, and it washed away about a half acre of our best river bottom land. Since then the river has calmed way down—taking a breather from gorging on our property.

The Land's history is interesting—at least to us. I just took a short course on geology of the Northwest from Bob Carson, who is a famous geologist and a professor at Whitman College here in Walla Walla. He had a lot of interesting stuff to say.

The way I understand it, way way back, The Land was probably part of an island out in the Pacific Ocean. Plate tectonics delivered the island to the general vicinity of where it is today about 150 million years ago give or take a few tens of millions of years. The Land crunched into North America and gradually settled in.

Starting about 17 million years ago and running for several million years, those old island rocks in this part of Washington State were mostly covered with lava flows from really long cracks in the earth that oozed the hot stuff all over the eastern half of the state, as well as much of Oregon and parts of Idaho. That far back, nobody was living around here, and that's good because it would have been an unpleasant place to be. This lava cooled into the basalt rock that pretty much sets the local geology. In places under Walla Walla and The Land, the basalt is a couple of miles deep.

About two million years ago, the Ice Age began. The glaciers in British Columbia and the mountains of Washington, Oregon and Idaho ground up the bedrock into silt-sized "rode flour." The glacial meltwater carried the silt down the Columbia River to places like the Pasco Basin just northwest of here and the Umatilla Basin just to the southwest. The prevailing winds from the Southwest picked up that fine-grained sediment and deposited it as loess (pronounced "luss") in the Palouse Hills just north of us. Any little puff of wind will blow this loess all over the place, and it is some of what you walk around on when you take a stroll across The Land.

From about 100,000 to 10,000 years ago (give or take a thousand years either way), the Earth was experiencing its most recent glaciation. A really big glacier covered all of British Columbia and slid down over into northern Washington, Idaho and Montana. As the glacier moved south it blocked rivers and created temporary lakes. One of the biggest of these lakes, called Lake Missoula, covered about 2,500 square miles of western Montana. In places it was 2,000 feet deep. This lake was held in check by a huge ice plug that would give way every few decades, and the entire lake would empty all over eastern Washington, picking up boulders and most of the soil as it roared through as a wall of water 900 feet high, moving along at 40 or 50 miles per hour. These floods are called the Missoula floods, and some Hollywood types are thinking about doing one of those natural disaster movies about them.

Most of the floodwater followed the route of the Columbia River which passes through a narrow gap in a basalt ridge called the Horse Heaven Hills just about 15 miles west of The Land. Well, that ridge is about 1,000 feet higher than the riverbed, and the gap (called Wallula Gap) through the ridge is pretty narrow, so the floodwaters would pile up at the gap waiting to get through, creating a big muddy temporary lake that backed up from the gap into the Walla Walla Valley and covered The Land in about 700 feet of water carrying a lot of sediment. While the muddy lake sat there, the sand and silt would settle out leaving a nice layer of dirt before the water managed to move through the gap.

Well, as if once wasn't enough, these floods apparently happened 80 to 100 times before things finally quieted down, leaving us with a valley full of good dirt. Since then, more loess has blown into the Walla Walla Valley and covered over the flood sediments.

Nobody knows if there were folks living around here during the floods. But it's a pretty fair bet that nobody survived the floods if they were here at all. Folks couldn't have moved in here and stayed until the floods ended about 13,000 years ago.

I'm still studying about the people that have lived on The Land, so I won't say too much here. I do know that in 1855, the US government took The Land from the local Indians (Cayuse, Umatilla and Walla Walla) and "donated" it in 1865 to a settler named Dauney who agreed to farm it. So, on the earliest maps of the valley, The Land is shown as part of the Dauney Donation Claim. Since then, the property has been mostly grazing pasture for cattle and horses.

The wildlife in the valley runs up a food chain from ground squirrels (that look and act a lot like prairie dogs) to quail, pheasant, turkey, some rabbits, white-tailed deer and the predators that feed on them—several kinds of falcons, hawks, golden eagles, barn owls, and

coyotes. There has even been one report of a cougar roaming the south edge of the valley down along the base of the ridge that separates Washington State and Oregon, and we're all hoping he stays down that way.

The Walla Walla River supports its own "riparian ecosystem" within the river and on its banks that ranges from plentiful minnows to smallmouth bass, bull trout, steelhead, salmon, and all kinds of birds including ducks and geese and big blue heron.

Our plan is to move the cattle off The Land and let the grasses grow up about waist high over the next few years, providing cover for the birds that will repopulate it. In the fall, we'll plant wheatgrass and wild ryegrass, sage, chokecherry, serviceberry, elderberry, willows, cottonwoods and ash down by the river to provide additional cover and food for the birds and foraging deer.

We'll fence off a section of The Land up in the northwest corner and build a small house, a guest cottage, a barn and fenced pastures for Annie's goats. Along with the goats (about which we know only what Annie has read in books and learned from her new online "goat lady" friends), we intend to have a few chickens, dogs and cats, an herb garden, a vegetable garden and a small patch of lavender, which apparently grows very well in our sandy soil.

The farmhouse will have a steel roof that swoops down to hang out over wide porches to protect us from the Walla Walla summertime sun and the sometimes heavy winter snows. The house will be constructed out of wood—mostly cedar reclaimed from massive six-story tall barns built by the State of Oregon back in the early 1900s down near Pendleton, Oregon. A big stone fireplace will open onto the front porch, which offers a spectacular view down the valley, beyond the lights of Walla Walla, to the foothills of the Blue Mountains.

My current favorite daydream features Annie and me sitting out on the porch in our big rocking chairs on a cool October evening watching the ducks and geese that fly around out there all the time, dogs at our feet and a big fire crackling in the fireplace between us. Another frequent daydream has family and friends scattered in small groups about the house and porches in the early evening, the ground still warm from the hot sunshine but the air cool and fresh, drifting in from the ridge tops to the south of us, a potluck of fruits, vegetables, breads and pies spread on the kitchen table, with hot dogs, ribs and hamburgers grilling outside.

According to the schedule, we won't be able to live

out these daydreams for at least another eight to nine months—around Christmastime if we're lucky. We can't wait to be there.

Well, I'm sure that's way more than you wanted to know about The Land but that's all I've learned so far. When I know more, I'll send you another letter unless you flag me down and say you've had enough. Annie says to tell Sharon and Angie we say hi.

Best,
Sam

Palouse Street House

May 2004

Dear Sally,

Annie tells me you and Frank were quizzing
her about our temporary quarters in Walla Walla. I
told her I'd write and bring you up to date. This may
be more than you want to know.

A few weeks ago, Annie and I rented a small 1920s
house on South Palouse Street, just a half block off
Main Street—our temporary home in Walla Walla
while we're waiting for the new house to get built. It's
owned by Jon (our architect) and Mary, his wife. We
can have it as long as we need it and they'll even let
our dogs and cats stay there.

Rein rings are still hooked into the curb in front of
the house where townsfolk and visiting farmers once
tied their horses while doing business in the shops
along Main Street. The house, which is wheat-colored
stucco with white trim, has a small front yard, a very
small covered front porch, a one-car garage off the
alley, and a tiny fenced backyard overlooking Mill
Creek. It has two small bedrooms, a bath, the littlest

kitchen you've ever seen, and a combination dining and living room that'll hold Annie and me and maybe one or two others if they're not too big. Marshall calls it a "Grandmother House," and to my way of thinking, that's about right.

Since we haven't moved from our house in Seattle yet, the furnishings at Palouse Street are sort of Spartan—and that's being generous. Our living room is furnished with one very old (and comfortable) club chair and a very uncomfortable straight-backed wooden dining chair—both facing a radio that sits plugged in on the floor across the room. On slow nights, I sit in the comfortable chair (if I get there first), Annie lies on the carpet with the dog and all three of us listen to Mariners baseball games. A bottle of local wine comes in handy.

In our dining room, we have what I call a "church supper table"—one of those indestructible, incredibly heavy steel-legged folding tables that you break bread over at spaghetti suppers. At the table, we have another straight-backed wooden dining chair. When we're both in town, we can steal the other dining chair from the living room and eat our dinners together—"intimate dining," I call it.

In the bedroom, I have one of those newfangled air-filled mattresses on the floor. I blow it up with an electric pump to the point of bursting (for maximum support). It's quite comfortable if you don't mind sleeping on what feels like a half-filled waterbed. Annie has a normal single bed mattress, also on the floor. She ditched her air mattress and hauled it off to the guest bedroom after one sleepless night. I'm sticking with my air mattress mostly because we spent a small fortune on it. She, on the other hand, feels no guilt leaving her air mattress to guests and hunkering down with an actual old-fashioned mattress. Rolling my 50-year old bones off that air mattress in the morning and moving to a standing position is a challenge but I'm getting better at it. It may not be pretty but it does provide some early morning amusement for Annie and the dog.

In an effort to look on the bright side, I call our little place in Walla Walla "romantic"—it reminds me a lot of our first years as a married couple. I tend to see it as a valuable exercise in downsizing. Annie's definition of romance varies somewhat from mine, but all in all we're pretty comfortable.

While we'd love for you guys to come visit, our little rental house may be too cozy for all of us to squeeze into. If you don't mind spending a few bucks, you could come over, stay at the Marcus Whitman Hotel (a first-class place), and you'd only be a few blocks from where we're living. So, think about it. If you're interested, let's pick a date and get you over here.

Best,
Sam

One Walla

This letter was written to yet another Larry. I know lots of Larrys and thought about trying to help you, the reader, keep them straight in your head until Annie told me that you wouldn't really care. I guess she's right. Just so you know, all the Larrys are different people.

Dear Larry:

I got your letter. Thanks.

Yes, the name really is Walla Walla. And yes, I know it's funny sounding. I thought so myself when I first heard it. I said to myself, "that is one funny sounding name"—just like you did. But now I guess I've heard it so much that I don't really notice it one way or the other.

I think your idea is actually a good one. I know you don't often have a good idea and Hotie tells me that you're a little sensitive about it, so I want to be sure to tell you when I think one of your ideas is good. Annie has been encouraging me to see the good in other people and to make more positive comments, so self-esteem will go up in the person complimented. It's

31

been a long time since I've heard a good idea out of you, so congratulations. And don't worry; I will give you full credit. I have to admit that I hadn't even thought of it myself before you mentioned it.

I agree that one Walla would be plenty. I don't know why they use two but I'll try to find out. And no matter what the reason, I'll let them know of all the good reasons you came up with to go with just one Walla.

I particularly like your idea on saving time. And I agree that there's got to be a way to figure out just how much time we can save; I have given it some thought and have this to offer. I'll be interested in what you think.

I have figured out how long it takes me to type two Wallas—about four seconds, sometimes five. I think I'm about an average typer, maybe a little on the slow side but not by much. So, if we divide 4 seconds by 2, we get 2 seconds to type one Walla. (I guess I could have just figured out how much time it takes me to type one Walla and that would have saved me some time but that's not the way I did it.)

OK, now I went to the Walla phone book and picked a page and counted the names. The print is really little but I'm pretty sure I got a good count. (I'm starting now to use just one Walla so I can start saving time, and maybe others will see it and start to do it and then it'll catch on everywhere.)

Now to be fair, I'm not sure that the page I picked has the same number of names as the average page but I don't want to spend any more time on trying to figure it out, so let's use 300 names per page. There are 96 white pages in the Walla phone book, so that's a total of 28,500 people in Walla and the surrounding area.

Annie has been looking over my shoulder and thinks this whole thing is stupid, but if I want to waste my time thinking about things like this, then she says I should just go to the Walla Chamber of Commerce where they will probably know how many people live in Walla. She's probably right, but I already figured it out this way. And I'm beginning to think Annie should follow her own advice and find some positive things to say to me.

So, how many times do you think the average Wallan types or writes or says the extra Walla each day? I'm guessing you'll say you don't know, so I'll just guess for both of us. I'll say 10 times each day. So that's 20 seconds each day that a person spends doing the extra Walla. (You can check my math when you get this letter and let me know where you think I'm off.) 20 seconds per day times 365 days per year is 7,300 seconds a year. That's 2.03 hours each year that a Wallan spends on the extra Walla.

Now if we multiply 2.03 hours times 28,500 Wallans, that's 57,855 hours a year that Wallans alone spend on the extra Walla. And that doesn't even count the non-Wallans that say or write or type the extra Walla. I can't even begin to think about how much time non-Wallans spend on the extra Walla each year, so I'm just leaving that out.

57,855 hours a year is a lot of time, and I think I'll take a copy of this letter to the mayor so he can see how much time could be saved. Just think of the increased productivity.

Annie is hungry and moaning that this letter needs to end so I can concentrate on fixing dinner. But I want to say again that I think you're really on to something with this extra Walla idea. We'll just have to see where it goes. I'll keep you posted. Please give our best to Hotie and tell her Annie says hello.

Best,
Sam

Footloose

Dear Ed:

You are right. We did rent that little house from our architect. It is on Palouse Street next door to the Christian bookstore and across the street from the electric shop. It is a cute little place and we have gradually been moving stuff over from Seattle so we can live there until the new house is done. This week I'm over here in Walla Walla with Babe (the dog) dealing with getting started on the new house while Annie deals with selling the old house. You asked how I am spending my time, and I'll have to say it beats the heck out of flying around the world on airplanes.

On Tuesday, Babe and I got up early (by our standards, not Walla Walla's). By 6:30 am I was cleaned up and Babe was fed and we were on Palouse Street headed to Merchants Delicatessen to find some breakfast. The air was fresh and cool. A light breeze blew, not a cloud in the sky. The streets were still pretty quiet.

Mill Creek runs west out of the Blue Mountains,

down through the foothills and right through town on its way to joining the Walla Walla River just west of town. Due to frequent flooding, the creek was switched over many years ago into a concrete flood control spillway that runs through the heart of downtown Walla Walla, some of it visible, and some underground. The spillway includes a fish ladder system to accommodate the trout and salmon that run up and down the creek at various times of the year. The creek runs under Palouse Street just a half block down from our rental house. As Babe and I walked over the bridge and looked down on the creek, we saw a huge bull trout finning its way downstream. "Wow," I said. Babe didn't seem to care; she was completely focused on our mission. "No delays," she seemed to say. "Let's get on to breakfast."

Babe and I love (and I mean, really love) food, just like you do—particularly breakfast. Annie's sort of like Sherril and couldn't care less about food; she eats only to maintain a fuel level barely above empty. Babe and I prefer to travel on a full tank. That is mostly why Annie is a slender little thing moving through life with two companions who appear well fed (I think that's the nicer way to describe us) and are always on the lookout for the next dining experience. Without Annie to distract or monitor us, Babe and I were on the big breakfast search.

At Main Street, we took a left and wandered past a small park where Fred was resting on a park bench with his bicycle leaning against his knees. In the short time we've been in town, checking in with Fred has become a part of our morning ritual. No matter where you're headed, you'll run into Fred along the way. Fred may not be the sharpest tack in the board anymore (apparently having something to do historically with too many drugs and too much rock 'n' roll), but he's one of the friendliest people on the planet. In spite of his raucous past, townsfolk have adopted Fred as one of their wayward children come home to roost, requiring some attention. Fred rides his bike around town from dawn to dusk almost every day waving at everybody he passes. Everybody loves Fred and waves back.

We spoke to Rachel who was hosing down the sidewalk in front of her furniture consignment shop and said hello to Tom who'd just opened up the new bagel place next door. It's hard to tell how well a bagel shop is going to do in the land of big breakfasts, but I hope their bagels catch on. It's well worth a wait if they've got some whole-wheat bagels coming out of the oven.

Another block down the street, we stopped to watch the road construction, which had been going on for several weeks. The road crew was finishing up a pretty tricky project that involved tearing out the heart of Main Street, replacing the utility guts of the town and putting it all back together without letting the street fall into Mill Creek flowing beneath it. Everybody seemed to agree that they were doing a masterful job.

Mr. Gray (who says he's 92 years old) was in his usual spot, sitting on the street bench watching the action with great interest. He must have retired from his road engineer's job at least 25 years ago, but takes a real, almost proprietary, interest in most any construction project happening in town.

"What's up, Mr. Gray?" I said.

"We're pouring cement today. Gotta shore up them supports to keep the street from falling into the creek," he replied without taking his eyes off either the cement truck shuttling its load into a cavity in the street or the crew boss who was orchestrating the fill.

"Sounds pretty important," I said.

"Is important," he said. "But no worries, we'll get 'er done today. It'll come out good."

"Well, I'm glad you're here watching over things," I said. "Thanks for all you're doing for the town."

"Not a problem. No thanks necessary," he replied, again without looking up from his supervisory duties.

Crossing the street, we almost collided with Betty who was out in front of her flower shop helping unload fresh flowers from her delivery truck. When Babe saw Betty, she almost jerked me off my feet. This was her shot at the next dining opportunity—almost a sure thing.

"Well, Babe! How are you this morning? Guess I know what you want," said Betty as she reached into the bottomless supply of dog treats that she keeps in her skirt pocket. Betty is Babe's new best friend; but let's be fair, anybody with a treat is Babe's new best friend.

Beneath a dark green awning, surrounded by planters full of geraniums, Merchants' sidewalk tables were already crowded with people. I said good morning to Bobbie who works down at the title company. She'd handled the closing on the purchase of The Land. She introduced me to the other ladies at the table as the "Seattle fellow who bought the old Lockwood place."

We all said our hellos and Bobbie offered to hang onto Babe while I went inside to order.

Merchants is sort of an institution. Bob, one of the owners, is an energetic sort who runs around the place doing everything from sweeping the floors to making gargantuan sandwiches to chatting up the regulars—and there are a lot of regulars. Bob's brother, and co-owner, Michael, bakes bread every morning in the back, so the place smells like your grandmother's kitchen, which encourages a healthy appetite. I ordered the plain omelet, ham, whole-wheat toast, tomato juice (to get my vitamins in for the morning) and a hot mug of Merchants coffee. Bob handed me a playing card, the King of Spades, and I wandered back outside to find a table.

There I saw that Bobbie and her friends had pooled their table scraps and were fixing to hand them down to Babe. For the last couple of months Annie and I, at the suggestion of our vet, have been working hard on controlling Babe's calorie intake and getting her some serious exercise. Babe is okay with moderate exercise as long as it's not too hot or too cold out. She hates her diet and whines pitifully after each meager meal. I don't think she's lost any weight and I'm guessing that our morning walks are part of the problem, not the solution.

Babe scarfed down those scraps before I could intervene. Babe knew I was coming and wasn't about to let me deprive her of more people food. Bobbie and her tablemates stared in awe. "I've never seen a dog eat that fast," said one of the ladies. "I've never seen any animal eat that fast, except maybe on Wild Kingdom," said another.

I thanked the ladies for watching Babe and Babe barked with excessive enthusiasm. We found a table down the way and settled in. In a few minutes, Jay, one of the waiters, wandered out onto the front porch toting my breakfast and barking "King of Spades, King of Spades." I flagged him down and settled in for a good half hour while I ate, drank my coffee and read bits and pieces of the various newspapers that the early risers had left for me. Babe lay down under my table but kept her eyes focused with some considerable intensity on the plates of the couple at the next table. This was a good eatery, and she wasn't going to miss anything coming her way.

After breakfast, Babe and I wandered back up Main Street. Mr. Gray was still at his post. Betty was outside chatting with one of the women working on the road crew. She started to reach in her pocket but I waved her off. "We're watching our figures," I called ahead, "and someday our diet is going to show some results." Betty snickered and said, "Sorry, Babe, maybe tomorrow." Babe had already had her bowl of doggie gruel, an early morning treat and a full plate of people food. She looked up at me and grumbled.

We got back to the house about 8:00 am. After a quick call to Greg, our builder, I settled in for a morning of reading about the history of Walla Walla and writing down what I'm learning about our new home. If productivity can be measured in words, I had a good morning.

By noon, I was starving. The last of the omelet's influence had fallen off. I needed a good healthy lunch—preferably with a glass of local wine of which there's plenty around here. Work a little bit, eat a little bit; work a little bit, eat a little bit. With practice, I felt like I could really get into this research and writing program. I wasn't sure yet about the quality of my writing, but I was quite sure about the quality of my appetite.

So, Babe and I went off in search of a great lunch spot. On a lark, we wandered down Second Avenue to Vintage Cellars, a great little wine bar. I had thought that it was open only in the evenings, but figured it wouldn't hurt to walk by just to make sure. Well, they were open, and Kelly was serving her special Greek salad to a couple of folks seated at the bar. She was happy for me to sit out on the deck where I was welcome to park Babe. Life was looking up.

Now, Kelly is one of the friendliest, perkiest bartenders you've ever met—a beautiful lady with sparkling brown eyes and an infectious smile who gets obvious pleasure from making her customers feel right at home. And, she's a fabulous cook. In my book, Vintage Cellars is a good place without folks like Kelly, but with them, it earns an extra star. It's a real shame that more places don't seem to understand that it's as much about the people as it is about the food or wine.

Anyway, I grabbed an empty table on the deck and waited for a menu. I knew what I wanted but it wasn't going to hurt to see what else Kelly was serving that day. We sat under an arbor covered over with canvas and wisteria. Daisies grew in pots along the fence railing. A surprisingly cool breeze came in from under the hot Walla Walla summer sun. It was 90+° on the street but at least 20° cooler on the deck. Nora Jones sang to me from hidden speakers. At that moment, it was one of the most pleasant places I'd ever been.

Soon Kelly showed up with a menu and a big bowl of water for Babe. She was recommending the Greek salad, so I went with that and a glass of whatever wine she chose. The salad was real fresh, made with local produce right off the farm—all organic, free-range, no MSG, etc. The wine was cool and crisp. It was terrific, but I forgot to ask what it was. Typical. I probably wouldn't have remembered the name anyway.

That lunch was special.

After I finished off my glass of wine, I left Babe under the table and went inside to pay my bill. Kelly took my money and asked what I was doing in Walla Walla. That led to the predictable discussion about our move to Walla Walla, why we were moving, where we were moving, when the house would be finished, and so on. She seemed genuinely interested, so I just rattled on, glad to have somebody to talk to.

After I'd bored her silly with my story, I picked up my change and headed for the door. Just as I opened it, Kelly called out, "Hey, Sam . . . before you go . . . Welcome to Walla Walla."

"Thanks, we're glad to be here," I said. And I really was glad to be in Walla Walla. It was starting to feel like home—a place where Annie and I could live out our dream.

So, Ed, get Sherril and the rest of your family and come on up for a visit. We promise you a good time.

Best,
Sam

Pass It On . . .

June 2004

Dear Gordon:

I really enjoyed seeing you and Kathy when I was in Nashville. I've been a sorry writer since, but you have been too, so I figure we're even. Dad says he saw you the other day and told you about our move to Walla Walla. Right now we expect to move into our new house around the end of the year. There'll be a guesthouse for you whenever you can find the time for a visit.

Dad says you were asking about what there is to do around Walla Walla. If we can get you off your Nashville behind and onto a plane to "the valley so nice they named it twice," we can tour some wineries, go to the rodeo if you come for Labor Day weekend, visit the Monteillet Fromagerie over in Dayton to sample some really good cheeses, visit the Pendleton Woolen Mills and wander around the town of Pendleton, do a little hunting or fishing, shoot some skeet or trap, tour the local art galleries, feed the goats, gather eggs, weed the garden, go to the Farmers Market on Saturday morning, chop some firewood, or do whatever else you want to do. I think we could keep you occupied for a few days.

One of the really refreshing things about Walla Walla is the friendliness. Everybody around here acts like you're their best friend whether they know you or not. I'm still surprised when somebody says hello to me like they've known me forever. At first I feel a little bad thinking that I've forgotten another face and wondering about my bad memory (and it really is pretty bad). Then I realize that they don't know me and I don't know them; they're just being friendly. Annie thinks it's real nice and I do, too.

You'll appreciate this little story, you being a man of the cloth and all. These sorts of mysterious things happen all the time around here.

One of the things we had to do before we could start building the new house was run a power line to the building site. This turned out to be right much more than we'd anticipated. The site is about three quarters of a mile from our little country road. Gene from the Columbia Rural Electric Authority came out and looked at the situation and quoted us a price that made me feel sick to my stomach. He was making us think twice about moving ahead. A few days later he called back with an idea. He said that there was power closer to the house site but running a line from that source would require laying an underground line across the alfalfa field of our neighbors to the west— the Belts. We'd have to get their approval, but if they'd let REA do it, we could save a lot of money.

Having arrived recently from a world where everything comes with a price, I asked Gene what the Belts would want to let us go that route. He said he knew Tom and his father, Ron. He'd check with them and get back to me.

A few days later Gene called back, said he'd talked to the Belts and they were happy to accommodate. I asked him what they wanted. He said "nothing"—said that Tom said letting us connect to power across their field was just the neighborly thing to do. Well, I'll say that Annie and I were astonished. What a nice thing to do; what a really nice thing to do. We didn't even know the Belts. We'd heard nice things about them and knew that they were our neighbors but we'd never met them. And here they were helping us out just because it was the right thing—the neighborly thing— to do. What a great place.

A few days ago, I got Tom's phone number so I could call, introduce myself, and maybe drop by and take them a little thank you gift. They weren't in so I left a message. Well yesterday I got a call back and had a real nice talk with him. He said again that they were just trying to help out. I'm going to stop by and see him sometime soon, but here's the mystical part that you'll like.

Yesterday afternoon on the same day that I'd finally caught up with Tom, I got a call from Austin, the local vet and the guy we bought The Land from. Austin said he had an unusual request for us and that we were sure free to say no if we didn't want to do it. He said he'd gotten a kind of emergency phone call from one of our neighbors up the road named Bill. Bill raises honeybees. This time of year he carts a lot of his bees over to Montana where he parks them in their hives on big fields where they pollinate the crops and make a load of sweet honey. Well, it's real dry over in Montana this year, so the crops aren't doing too well and neither are the bees. Bill was so worried about them that he'd loaded them back on his truck and was bringing them back to Walla Walla even thought he had no place to put them. So, Austin was asking for Bill whether we'd be willing for him to put them on our land for a few months until he moves them to a new home in September.

I said I'd talk to Annie but I thought that'd be just fine. Annie and I talked it over and decided that it was just the neighborly thing to do and that it was interesting how we had the chance to do something for a neighbor right after the Belts had done such a nice thing for us. But I'm sure it comes as no surprise to you.

So, Bill is moving his bees onto The Land early tomorrow morning. He asked us what we'd want for letting him do it. I said nothing; glad to help out; but he said they were going to bring us some honey all the same. It'll be interesting to taste honey made from the wildflowers on our Land.

Anyway, I thought you'd like the story. It was a good reminder to us to help out where we can. Pass it on . . .

Best,
Sam

It Ain't a Truck

June 2004

Dear Tony:

You'll get a kick out of this. We bought the truck; I mean, "rig." We have a rig now, so we can hold our heads up while riding around Walla Walla.

Shortly after we bought The Land, I was out there with Jay. I first met Jay a couple of years ago when I looked at investing in his winery. Well, I didn't invest and as a consequence, the winery seems to be doing real well. Seems like that's always the way. I'm telling you that someday I'm going to write a book advising people on what I'm buying and selling. It should be a bestseller. Anybody buying it will make a killing if they just do the opposite of what I do. If I'm buying, then you should sell and vice versa.

Well anyway, the point is that I met Jay and got to know him a little bit. I learned that one of his businesses was working with landowners on fixing up stream banks and other environmental projects. So when Annie and I bought The Land, I called Jay and asked if he could help me figure out the best way to turn our pastures into a good place for wildlife. He said sure and met me out at the property one afternoon to have a look around.

We spent a good while talking beside his truck when it dawned on me that he was having a much easier time driving around the property in his truck than I was in my Volvo sedan. No roads, ground squirrel mounds, tall grass and shrubs—hey, maybe I needed a truck. So, I asked him where I should go look for a truck. Jay laughed and said, "You mean a rig; it ain't a truck, it's a rig." "Okay," I said. "Where should I go look for a rig?"

Well, that opened up a new gate. We spent more time that day talking about rigs than we did about The Land. Jay loves his rig and has a lot to say about it.

We talked about diesels versus gas engines, Chevy versus Dodge versus Ford, short beds versus long beds, 4 wheel drive versus 2 wheel drive, crew cabs versus single cabs, etc., etc., etc. It turns out that there's a lot of important stuff to know about rigs. Well, it was a start. For the next couple of weeks I asked everybody I met what kind of rig they had and what they'd recommend for a neophyte farmer like me. If you ever decide to move to Walla Walla, I'd highly recommend that you always mention that you're thinking about getting a rig; it's a real icebreaker.

It will come as no surprise to you that everybody had a different idea about what kind of rig we needed. (I don't know if the word "need" is really the right one.) And it was real confusing until I realized that it was like ordering coffee.

Remember when you ordered coffee and the only

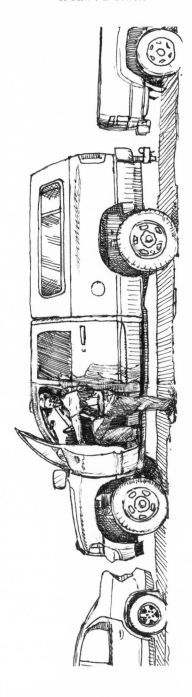

real choice you had was cream or no cream? So, now you have to know a lot more to order coffee but we've all gotten used to it. Well, figuring out what rig you want is like learning about ordering coffee. So, after all the talk, we got a "Dodge diesel one-ton, crew cab, short bed, automatic, with running boards, spray-in bedliner, canopy cover, running lights, fog lamps, and 6-CD player."

And here are the answers to all those questions I know are rolling around in your head:

Q: Why a Dodge?

A: It was cheaper. After we added up all the rebates, throwaways, cutbacks, and 0% financing, it was just plain cheaper than the Ford or Chevy.

Q: Why a one-ton?

A: I still don't really know the difference between a half-ton and a one-ton. You'd think the one-ton would be twice as big, but it isn't. I think it has something to do with how much you can tow because I remember somebody telling me that you can tow a whale with the one-ton and you won't even know it's back there. (Well, I sort of doubt that but it sounded impressive.) So, we got the one-ton. That's all I know to tell you.

Q: Why the diesel?

A: Well, that's another good question. At the end of the day we got the diesel because if you take care of them they'll go 300,000 or 400,000 miles before you have any big problems with them. I drive maybe 10,000 miles in a good year so this truck should last us a good 30 to 40 years if we take care of it. I'll be long dead by the time I ever have to buy another vehicle and that seemed like a selling point to me. Also, the diesels don't have catalytic converters like gas engines. Catalytic converters get real hot after you drive for a while. If you park a rig with a hot catalytic converter in a field of tall dry grass you can set off a grass fire and burn up the whole county. I understand the neighbors don't like that, so that's another reason to get the diesel—we're less likely to burn down the place we're moving to—another selling point.

Q: Why the crew cab?

A: This was Annie's answer: For toting the grandchildren around when they all come to visit. I think you'll remember that we have three daughters so there's potential for grandchildren. But right now that's all we've got is potential. We don't have any grandchildren or even any husbands at this point. These are minor points according to Annie, so we needed a crew cab. Hey, I know it doesn't make any sense, but you have to pick your battles.

Q: Why the fog lamps and running lights?

A: Now this is maybe the best question you've asked. This rig is huge. Big trucks pull way off to the side to let us pass. And the diesel engine makes a racket like it's going to blow up at any moment. I can't believe that there could be anybody out there who wouldn't know we were coming. But just in case they're not paying attention, they'll now be able to see our glow on the horizon long before they spot or hear our rig.

Q: Why the 6-CD player?

A: Beats me. Ask Annie. She'll tell you something that'll sound reasonable until I tell you that a diesel is so loud that you have to pull into a rest area and turn off the engine to listen to your CDs. Go figure.

So, there you go. We got a rig. And now we can drive around sort of looking like we fit in. And if anybody ever asks us to haul a whale for them, we'll be able to help out.

Write when you can. Annie loves mail. And tell Judy we say hi.

Best,
Sam

PS: My daughter, Jolie, read this before I sent it to you and said she thought it was funny that I ended the letter "Best, Sam." Of course that is just short for "Very Best Regards, Your Devoted Friend, Sam McLeod" and anything else you'd like to add to it. I figure folks can understand that.

But she says that's not her point. She says that I could just shorten it further and just use "BS". She thinks that'd be a more fitting end to my letters. Well, ha ha, Jolie. I think you're very funny. I'm just laughing out loud.

So, anyway, I'm sticking with "Best, Sam."

S

Women Only

June 2004

Dear Tommy:

It was good to hear from you. Glad to hear that Bradley and Kristin are doing so well. Please give Becky our best.

By the way, you were right about the goats. This is quite an adventure. Annie has already bought four goats and we don't even have a place to put them yet. Thankfully, the lady who sold them to her can keep them until we have a barn and some fenced pasture—probably in late December.

Annie must have about ten books on goats—raising them, milking them, shearing them, selling them, etc. There's a lot to know—way more than I would have imagined—but Annie is into goats big time. She already has a bunch of goat lady friends who are constantly chattering with her about goats, answering all her questions.

We're not pursuing the milk goat idea right now. Once we figured out the time required to milk them twice a day for seven to eight months of the year and the amount of cheese we'd have to make, we backed off and Annie started looking at angora goats instead. Right now, that's where we're headed. Angoras are raised for their "fiber" and for meat—not milk. So, they're a little less work. They're also a little smaller and less rambunctious than most of the milk goats which makes them easier to manage.

Basically we'll have to water them and pasture them every day, but otherwise leave them alone, unless we're helping the new mothers drop their kids (yep, that's what they call giving birth in the goat world), worming them, tending to a sick one, giving them their vitamins or trimming their hooves. At least for now, we'll get somebody else to shear them and butcher the meat goats.

One very interesting thing about the goat world—it's pretty much a women's game. Everybody Annie has met in the business is female and they run the show. Yeah, they may be married and their husbands may help out some, but the women run everything (except maybe the butchering of the kid goats which they don't seem to care for).

The other interesting thing is that it's the same way with the goats too. The women goats are called "does" and they do most everything. They have the baby goats (called kids), raise them up and produce the mohair fiber they're famous for. The men goats are called bucks and are only good for one thing. They just do their job for a few days in the fall each year and then are sent off to a pasture by themselves until their turn comes up again the next year. They don't even get to socialize with the does and kids in the meantime. Annie says they're mostly "ostracized" and are not much a part of goat society. (I'm going to have to look that word up for what it means and spelling but maybe you've heard it before.)

Now if you're born a boy goat this all means that you'd better arrive in the world very good looking with a full body of great hair. In this business it's all about the hair and looking good. A really good looking male kid has got a good shot at avoiding an early trip to the butcher and may even avoid castration, and I think that's where you want to be. You'll probably be sold off and sent packing to a new family when you're about 9 months old and you'll have to get to know a whole new group of goats, but that's way better than a trip to the meat locker. And who knows, there may be some cute young does in your new group so there's some upside.

If you're a baby boy goat and you're good looking but not great looking, you may avoid an early trip to the butcher, but you'll get your balls cut off (or they'll put a tight rubber band around them when you're a little guy and they'll shrivel up). It gives me the shivers every time those goat ladies start talking about castration like it's no worse than getting a flu shot.

Once your balls are gone, you're not a buck anymore. Then they call you a wether. Don't ask me where they got that name; I don't know. (They could have used eunuch or gelding or another word, but no, they have to have their own word.) They'll shear your hair twice a year and let you hang out with the real buck to keep him from getting lonely. I guess you probably have a kind of inferiority complex and you must get lonely yourself when the real guy is sent in with the does in the fall. Maybe they let you baby-sit the kids while the real buck is servicing the moms (yep again, that's what they call it—a service). You never get to hang out with the does or the kids unless this babysitting gig works. I'll have to ask Annie about that. The only really good news is that if you come in runner up in the beauty contest, you avoid that trip to the big butcher block.

Now, if you're born a boy goat and aren't all that good looking, then you'd better get on with living your life to the fullest and try to stay real skinny, because when you hit about 70 pounds on the barn scale, you're headed down the road to the butcher. There's a big and growing market for kid goat meat and you don't want to be part of it. The catch is that living your life to the fullest means all you do is eat. (Goats don't drink, they don't smoke and there's no sex for the not-so-good looking). If all you do is eat, that'll run you up to 70 pounds pretty fast. So, the big and unsolved problem for baby boy goats that are a little on the homely side is how to enjoy your life while fasting. I'd never make it myself.

I hate to get psychological on you but learning this makes me wonder a little bit about where Annie is headed with this goat thing. For the first time it hit me that there's a strange coincidence going on here. When Annie and I got married, I had a boy dog named JB and a boy cat named Ralph. Ralph was a great cat but ended up being part of a long, sad story when he caught and played with a rabid bat one day. We had to take him to the SPCA and have him put down. JB ended up going to live on a big farm outside of Charlottesville with some friends when Annie and I moved off to the big city of Chicago where JB would not have been a very happy dog.

Those were the last boys that were ever part of our family. Since then we've had two female cats, three female children, two female birds (I don't remember what kind), a bunch of female gerbils (after we culled out the males for doing their job too well), two female dogs and two more cats that are in the "used to be male" category. I am the only real boy in this whole crowd.

Now I am going to live on a farm where we're going to raise female goats and a few dogs (probably female unless I start lobbying hard now). This thinking has made me a little nervous around rubber bands and knives. I hate it when the goat ladies start talking about culling the bucks that are getting on in years. I'm getting on in years myself. Maybe I've thought on it too hard and should stop worrying, but I don't really know.

Anyway, I hope you're all doing real well. Write to me when you can.

Best,
Sam

PS: Since I wrote this letter, we have acquired another dog. Thank goodness, he's a boy—at least for a while until the ladies in my family have a big meeting about it and decide that he'd really be better off if we got him "fixed."

His name is Yoda. He's a little Corgi, about 10 weeks old with these really big Yoda-like ears. All the ladies call him "cute" and "adorable" which is nicer than "funny looking." I think he's just funny looking myself—not as nice, but the honest truth. He is mostly a good little dog unless he starts imagining you're a sheep or a goat or some other animal that needs herding, and he starts nipping at your heels. Those little teeth are sharp if he grabs you just right. But back to the point, we have another boy in the family now and we're sticking together for mutual protection. Neither of us wants to get fixed.

S

Horses

June 2004

Dear Hal:

I hope you and Mary had a good trip and enjoyed the horseback riding at the Boulder River Ranch. We love that place. I thought I'd write to tell you about Marshall's horse show in Oklahoma City. I know you're a horse person and might be interested. There are horse people everywhere here in Walla Walla, so I'm trying to pay more attention to this horse showing business myself.

Annie and I went down last week to the big Appaloosa Horse Show that goes on for about two weeks. It's in this huge coliseum with way more seats than are required for the moms and dads that are there to see their daughters ride. There are some friends and extended family members in the crowd but you know it's their first year to see the show because, I think it's safe to say, they wouldn't choose to go back a second time.

I think they use that big coliseum because whoever runs the place will let those horse people fill it up with dirt for the horses to run on and do their business on.

Anyway, Marshall loves riding horses like you do. I think she'd pretty much rather ride than do most anything else except "hang out" with her boyfriend (whatever that means, I'm not quite sure). She does western pleasure riding where, near as I can understand it, the whole point is to ride a horse and get it to do a bunch of stuff it wouldn't normally choose to do while the rider tries to look like she's not doing anything. I think the rider must get points for looking bored and maybe even a few more points for nodding off occasionally. At least that's the way I see it. Marshall is pretty darned good at looking like she's doing nothing when she's just hanging around the house, so I can see where she'd have a real talent for this horse riding.

Well, I have to say that it's not much of a spectator sport. I go to be supportive but not because of the adventure and daredevil excitement. One of the other dads there said that watching about 500 girls do the same thing in that big ring where they're all trying to look like they're doing nothing puts him to sleep. Well I mean to tell you that the moms just jumped all over him for being insensitive and a clod but near as I can tell he was just saying what every other spectator (including the moms) was thinking. Another one of the dads said that sitting about 12 hours every day for two weeks to watch this western riding was only marginally better than watching ice melt but he was smarter than the other dad and didn't say it where any moms could hear him. But I'll tell you all the dads that heard him nodded like they understood exactly what he meant.

Well, Marshall did real well and won a bunch of ribbons and had all kinds of people taking her picture and congratulating her, so I think she had a lot of fun. Annie was just as proud as a puffed up peacock. And I can say I'm real proud of her, too.

Sometimes if nothing important was going on, Annie and Marshall would get me to hold her horse's reins while they were off studying for the next event. Well, I hate to admit this to someone like you who loves horses, but big animals scare me silly. I don't know what they're thinking other than I'd like to stomp this guy into the ground. I don't like holding anything tied to an animal bigger than I am. As you know, Annie and I are moving to a farm over in Walla Walla, Washington, but I only agreed to do it if Annie agreed that we'd never own any animals bigger that we are. Anyway, I'd stand there looking real stupid and not having any idea what I'd do if the horse did decide to stomp me into the ground. Marshall told me once that her horse, Tammy, likes peppermint candy so I raided the candy jar in our hotel room and put a bunch of mints in my pocket just to deal with events like this. I figure if you're feeding a big animal her favorite food, that'll reduce the number of bad thoughts she's having about stomping you.

Like I said, most of the parents have no clue what's good riding or bad riding. One day last week, I arrived at the arena when they were doing something called showmanship. There were about 55 girls in this class all about to do the same thing over and over. I asked one of the other dads to point out a good go when he saw one so maybe I could see it done right and would be able to tell if Marshall did well when her turn came around. Well, this guy straightened up in his seat and tried to look real knowledgeable. We watched several of these kids do the same thing—one looking just like the other to me—when Len leaned over and said that number 1106 had just had a very good go. And that I should pay attention to what she'd done. Well about two hours later they'd all had their turns. Everybody agreed that Marshall had looked real good but that she'd "broke" on her last diagonal. I didn't know what that was but it didn't sound too good. As all the riders came back into the arena, Len leaned over again and very official-like told me that he'd be very surprised if 1106 hadn't won it all.

So, they started calling out numbers in reverse order of place so the girl that won 10th place came out before 9th place and so on. Well, you just couldn't believe how excited Len was getting as they called out numbers and 1106 wasn't among them. He said that was because she was going to get first place. When they got to third they called out Marshall's number and we all whooped and hollered for her real big. Then they called out 2nd place and it wasn't 1106. Now Len was about to pee in his pants he was so excited. After we'd all whooped for number 2, Len puffed out his chest and started pointing to number 1106 and mouthing to everybody that she was going to be the champion. Then the announcer said, "and here's our world champion, she's number 1106 Miss So and So riding Such and Such from Somewhere" and Len was out his seat doing his version of a victory dance. Not only was he proud of picking the winner, but he was clearly ecstatic that he finally knew good riding from bad.

He was accepting congratulations all around when the announcer said to whoa up a minute. There'd been a big mistake and the winner wasn't 1106, it was 1160. Well another big whoop went up for number 1160 and Len took his chance to sit back down just like nothing had happened and acted like he couldn't hear all of us dads sitting behind him just laughing out loud. One of the other dads yelled out to Len that "pride goeth before the fall" and said we all should learn something from Len's embarrassment. That was a fun time had by all except Len, and the highlight of showmanship for me.

Anyway, hope I didn't bore you too much with all this. Let us know when you two can come out to the West for a visit. It'll take you about two days of steady driving to get out here and the same going back so I'd suggest you plan to spend some time here, and then take in some other places out in this part of the world.

And yes, we did get that little dog we were telling you about. A family from Texas that was showing horses had also brought along a litter of little Corgi puppies. I'm not much of a little dog fan, but over the course of several days Annie, Marshall and I got won over by this little male Corgi named Yoda (because he has huge Yoda-like ears). So, Annie couldn't stand it and said if we'd get him, she'd take care of him and figure out how to keep him in our hotel room, and feed him, and clean up after him and then how to get him on a plane and get him home. Well, I've made this mistake before and should know better, but I said okay, took my extra points for being a good husband,

and wrote the check.

He is a real cute little guy but he is chewing up everything in sight. So, like everybody, he has got his good and bad points. But we love him, so I guess we did the right thing.

Best,
Sam

Inhabitants

June 2004

Dear Randy:

Wow. Since we told people we were moving to Walla Walla and I started writing folks to get more connected in my life, we have gotten a flood of mail full of questions that we mostly can't answer—at least not yet. Annie is loving this. She loves to get mail and the more the better. She can't wait to open our water and sewer bill so you can imagine how excited she gets over real mail. She claims that she has been first in line at the post office every day for the last week. I tell her it's an admirable achievement and that maybe she can set some sort of world, or at least Walla Walla, record and get her name in the newspaper. We'll see.

I'm telling you all this because I don't have answers to all the questions you sent us. I'm working on them, but I'm not there yet. And no, I don't think the whorehouses are still operating but I have not been by to check. Maybe you can look into this when you come to visit next spring.

Now, about your regular history questions, I have

tried to put them together in a chronological way and answer them in an order that we can all understand. I talked to a fellow over at Whitman College (so I guess he'd know or at least he'd know enough to make it up good if he doesn't know everything for sure). I asked him about the first people settlers of the Walla Walla Valley. He says that folks wandered over here to the Pacific Northwest from Asia sometime around 20,000 years ago. When the last Ice Age was going strong, so much water froze up on land that the oceans went down enough to open up a strip of land in the Bering Strait that made it easy for the folks to come on over to North America from Siberia by way of Alaska. Well, as you probably know, some went east, some went south and some settled in our part of the world.

Nobody knows for sure when folks actually moved into the Walla Walla Valley, but they guess around 13,000 years ago. The reason they don't know more is that those big Missoula Floods poured through here pretty regularly and wiped everything clean until about 13,000 years ago. Any folks that moved in between floods would have waked up one day to see about 700 feet of water pouring in on top of them, and they and everything they owned would have been relocated down the valley and on into the Columbia River Gorge down in Oregon.

You might be interested in reading up on the Marmes rock shelter that was found on the Palouse River just north of Walla Walla before it was dammed back in 1969. Folks found all kinds of bones, weapons, and even a sewing needle there, and figured out that people had been living there around 10,000 years ago. Those folks might have known the famous Kennewick Man whose remains were found just about 40 miles east of the Marmes cave. So, let's just say for purposes of moving on with our story that this area didn't get settled by the first North Americans until about 13,000 years ago—when The Land was home to mastodons, wooly mammoths, saber-toothed tigers, and beavers the size of bears.

Nowadays, where we are living is pretty dry—just seven or eight inches of rain in most years. So folks settling in around here stuck pretty close to the rivers—the Columbia, the Snake and our own little Walla Walla. That way they could get water, do some fishing for salmon and feed on the plants that grew along the riverbanks. Over time these people formed into Indian tribes that became the Walla Walla, the Cayuse, the Nez Perce and the Umatilla.

By the early 1800s, local Indian tribes had acquired horses and were using them to hunt beyond the river valleys for deer and elk and bear. The Walla Walla, Cayuse, Nez Perce and Umatilla regularly traded with other tribes in what is now Washington State, and also with the European traders that moved up and down the Columbia River. The Indians lived in lodges that housed as many as ten families under one roof, and they shared virtually everything they possessed. Tribes tended to live and hunt in an area defined by the limits of horse travel, but there was no concept of land ownership as we know it.

According to some local folks, the Walla Walla and Cayuse fished the Walla Walla River stretch that sets the north border of the Land. It is said that they dried their catches on the rise that runs from west to east along the ancient riverbed just below where we are building our new house.

Lewis and Clark showed up in the Walla Walla Valley in 1806 on their way back to the East Coast. They hung out with the Indians around here and explored the area just west of The Land. For the most part, they found the Indians helpful and hospitable.

In 1812, Fort Nez Perce was built by the Pacific Fur Company in Astoria, Oregon. The fort was really just a trading post set up to trade with tribes in the area. In 1813, the British-owned North West Company bought the fort, and the trading post was moved to the east bank of the Columbia River near the mouth of the Walla Walla River. In time the name was changed to Fort Walla Walla. In 1821 it was bought up by the Hudson's Bay Company.

By the way, I found out why Walla Walla has two Wallas. Apparently the word "walla" means water or small stream in the language of the local Indians. So, "walla walla" means many waters or many small streams, and probably refers to the creeks and small rivers that run down out of the Blue Mountains into the Walla Walla River before it dumps its water into the Columbia.

Well, the arrival of white folks was not a very good thing for the Indians. Between 1844 and 1854, what had been a trickle of settlers quickly turned into a flood. By the mid-1800s diseases like measles had taken a terrible toll on tribes in the Walla Walla Valley, and white settlers were moving into the area in ever growing numbers, setting up fences, bringing their animals, growing their crops and generally taking the place over.

Marcus and Narcissa Whitman had shown up in the Walla Walla Valley and set up their mission just down the road from The Land. Marcus Whitman was the only doctor between Fort Laramie and the end of the Oregon Trail. So his mission became more of a hospital than a church school. That meant that a lot of sick people showed up around here looking for medical help. And that meant that the local tribes were continually exposed to the worst diseases the white man had to offer.

It was after a serious measles epidemic that some of the local Indians had had enough and killed the Whitmans and other whites at the mission in 1847, believing that the missionaries were responsible for the sickness. Well, that set everybody off and there was trouble between the Indians and whites for about the next ten years until Washington, DC flexed its muscles, sent in the troops and basically forced the local tribes to accept a treaty that called for the Indians to give up their lands and move onto a reservation.

As a result, our government was holding all this land that it couldn't do anything with so it turned around and gave the land to settlers who'd agree to farm it. So, in December of 1865, the government gave The Land to a couple named Dauney and they started farming it. I haven't gotten down to figuring out which families have lived on The Land since then but will work on it and get back to you.

Well now, since I've written up all these events, Annie is starting to worry. (She's always worrying over something so it might as well be this.) She's afraid somebody will show up and kick us off The Land just like our government did to the Indians. We've always known that we'd only have it for a short time but never thought about forcible ejection, or massive floods, or massacres, or the like.

I guess anything's possible but it's not way up on my list of things to fret about. What I do know though is if they come to kick us off and they're bigger than us, it's best to not put up too much of a fight. Fighting back hasn't seemed to pay off too well for the folks that were here before us. Maybe when it's your time, it's your time and you should just go peaceably—better kicked off than tortured and dead is the way I see it.

I hope you'll think about all this and write me back. I'd be interested in your ideas. And Annie'll have something to pick up when she goes early to get her #1 spot at the post office. Tell everybody down there in Florida we say howdy. (Now that we live in Walla Walla we don't say hi anymore. Saying howdy makes me feel like a cowboy and I'm into that.)

Best,
Sam

Onions on the
Fourth of July

July 2004

Dear Gary:

I hope this letter gets to you before you take off on your big hiking trip. Mom tells me that you'll be hiking the Appalachian Trail for a month with Brian and that you won't be back in Nashville 'til mid-August. Well, it sounds like a lot of hard walking with 50 pounds on your back, sweating to beat the band, eating a lot of stuff out of foil pouches, and lying on the ground to sleep, with mosquitoes keeping you awake all night. I'm sure glad you like it. Everybody's different.

Well, it's onion time around here. There are loads of folks in the fields all around town pulling up onions all day long. There are big bags of onions for sale everywhere, and I mean everywhere—every store, every gas station, roadside stands, on the sidewalks, at the Farmers Market—everywhere. I even saw several bags hanging from a flagpole alongside the American Flag this morning like it's the thing to do around here on Fourth of July.

Now, I'll have to say that I didn't really know much

about Walla Walla Sweet Onions until a few days ago. Before that I was like you, from Nashville, where the only onions anybody talks about are Vidalia onions from Georgia. Well, I now think Walla Walla Sweets are better. You can take a bite out of a raw onion and it's just as mild and sweet as you can imagine.

People around here are crazy for 'em. In the fall, Jolie works part-time as a teacher's assistant at one of the local elementary schools, mostly helping first graders with their reading skills. She tells me that one day she was standing with several little six-year-olds in the cafeteria line when the cafeteria lady asked one of the little boys if he wanted onions on his hamburger. Well, this little boy, probably about three feet high, just pipes right up and says, "Are they Walla Walla Sweets? 'Cause that's all I eats is Walla Walla Sweets." You know they're something when six year olds will eat 'em.

So, about lunchtime today, Babe and I decided we'd take a walk and strike out for town to find some lunch. Annie is off with Marshall and Yoda down in Oregon where Marshall is riding her horse in a show. Anyway, it was just me and Babe and there wasn't much in the fridge so we figured we'd walk downtown to Vintage Cellars for a salad and a glass of wine. Well, I mean to tell you there was nobody downtown. Other than a couple of people sitting out in front of Starbucks, it was a ghost town—sort of eerie—nothing open and no people around. Signs on almost every door said Closed for the Fourth of July.

Finally I found a guy coming out of his office and locking up his door, so I just up and asked him where everybody was. He said, "Pioneer Park." Okay, so I know where the park is and it's not too far from our little rental house, so we walked back to the house and got Babe some water before walking up to Pioneer Park to see what was going on. It was a gorgeous day—probably 85 degrees and not a cloud in sight.

Well, as we got within a few blocks of the park every house along the road was decked out in American flags, red white and blue bunting, and those whirly things that spin in the wind. Folks were all out on their front porches eating and drinking iced tea. Bunches of kids were playing in front yards in plastic blow-up pools and running all over with their dogs chasing after them. Tables were loaded down with chicken and deviled eggs and potato salad and all manner of other stuff. In each yard there was a bunch of guys huddled around the grill doing hamburgers and hotdogs. My it looked good, and I'm afraid Babe and I were drooling so people could see. One nice lady even stopped us and asked if she could get Babe some water. Mighty nice of her.

The park was full of people but not really crowded. Families were scattered around with big picnic spreads, lots of coolers, blankets on the ground and lawn chairs in abundance. There was a group on stage playing Fourth of July music. It was right out of a Norman Rockwell picture. Annie would have loved it so I'm sure we'll go next year and probably every year after that. Little booths were set up right through the middle of the park selling everything from sno-cones to corn on the cob to burgers and dogs to local crafts and foods. Well, that's when I noticed it—onions were everywhere here, too. Stands sold onion relish, pickled onions, onion sauces and onion dressings. One booth sold big fried onions and onion rings. Onions were prepared pickled, baked, fried, and grilled and probably other ways that I didn't see—whole, quartered, sliced and diced.

And I just had to try it all. I'm telling you those pickled Walla Walla Sweet onions were good. I ate grilled Walla Sweets on a big bratwurst with lots of mustard. And I couldn't resist one of those fried onions—way more than I could eat but absolutely sweet and delicious. One little place had done onions and tomatoes baked in aluminum foil serving bowls, served cold. They were my favorites—like eating dessert.

Sorry to run on about onions, but they are big stuff around here and I'm hooked on them.

Maybe instead of going hiking next year you could come out here and we could hike around town eating onions. I'm told there's even a big onion festival here around the end of July. I'll let you know.

Best,
Sam

PO Box

July 2004

Dear Brian:

Thank you for your letter. Annie loves mail and we both enjoyed reading about your new business. It sounds like you're really enjoying meeting all those new folks and flying around all the time, but I'll have to say that I'm sure not envying you all that travel. After 30 years of flying around on airplanes, I've put airplanes on the "been there, done that" list. Since we've moved over here to Walla Walla, I've gotten worse about flying and have cancelled two trips just because I don't ever want to sit in one of those little seats again if I can help it. My new truck was built for somebody even wider than me and has plenty of room. So I'm just exploring around here instead of running off to Tahiti or some other place. Hope you can get over here for a visit sometime.

Well, we finally got a post office box yesterday, so I guess our move over here is official. The Walla Walla Post Office is right on Second Avenue as you come into town on the highway, so it's very convenient. While we could get our mail out at the farm, we're so far off the road and gone so much that we figured we'd get our mail in town so we don't have to worry about it stacking up.

Plus, lots of folks around here have PO boxes so you see your neighbors when you're at the post office. I've already met a bunch of folks in line waiting to mail out a package or something. You know, it's real interesting to watch folks around here. In the city, folks in line are like caged animals harrumphing and tapping their feet. It's right unpleasant. But here, being in a line is like going to a party. Everybody's talking about getting in the wheat, or their kids, or the heat, or whatnot.

Two older ladies in front of me the other day got into an interesting conversation about putting up green tomato pickles and onion relish that somehow meandered to the gas problems that such condiments can foster. I think her name was Mildred and she obviously was a little hard of hearing, so when she talked, she could reach the other end of town with whatever she was saying. I'm quite sure that her husband Bill would not have been too excited to hear her telling about his nighttime gas. But everybody around now knows that Mildred doesn't serve anything pickled except at outdoor picnics and family gatherings where she has to—and then only if she knows she can sleep down the hall in the guest bedroom.

Well, when I got up to the counter to get a PO Box, this nice young lady with a big smile on her faced asks what she could do to help me. Can you believe it? She works for our government and she's smiling and she's asking if she can help. I don't think I've ever seen that before but it was a real nice change.

Turns out there are five different sized boxes you can choose from, numbered from Size 1 which is the smallest to Size 5 which is a great big thing that you could stuff a sofa pillow in. Well, Susan (that's the nice lady's name) says there's a lot to decide in picking out a PO Box, which was a surprise to me. And she was going to tell me all the options. Annie is reading this looking over my shoulder and thinks nobody's interested in knowing about how I got a PO Box but I'm thinking she's wrong because around here folks will talk about the most regular things and since I retired and have time, those things are interesting to me. So, you'll have to write back and tell me whether you liked this letter or were bored silly.

Anyway, the first thing you have to decide on is the size box you want. Now I've always been in the bigger-is-better camp on things and immediately jumped to asking her about a Size 3 box figuring we could start there and work up. Well, Susan says whoa down just a minute and, even though there's right smart of a line forming up behind me, she says we should start with a Size 1 box which will hold a bunch of regular size letters and other small stuff but isn't, in her opinion, very good if you get a bunch of magazines. Well, we aren't much on magazines but Annie is a big fan of catalogues from all kinds of places, so I had to tell Susan that we should go on to box Size 2 because there's no way Annie is giving up her potty reading.

Susan got right tickled at that and said she'd never heard catalogues called potty reading and turned over to the other lady next to her named Patty and asked her if she'd ever heard that and she said no, but

Harold in line waiting behind me says his family has always called catalogues and The Upper Room and Reader's Digest and such potty reading. And then the lady in line behind Harold chimes in that her grand-dad spends so much time on the pot that they call him Grandpot even to his face because he can't hear anything. And she's been wondering what to get her granddad for Christmas and now she's thinking that she's going to needle point up a sign for him to hang by the toilet above his little bookstand in there saying "Potty Reading." Well, I wished I'd never said it 'cause the line was getting longer behind me and we were off course on getting a PO Box. Plus it's going to be interesting when somebody asks Annie about her potty reading; I'm sure I'll hear about it and it won't an uplifting experience.

Anyway, a Size 2 box is big enough for letters and a reasonable amount of catalogues, says Susan. So that got us going on what's a reasonable amount of catalogues. Now, I'm not a catalogue person, and spend my catalogue time throwing them away into the recycling without so much as looking at the cover. So any number of catalogues is unreasonable in my mind. But Annie likes catalogues like she likes presents—the more the better—and gets real excited when she can catch one before I can throw it out. Sometimes I find a big stack of ones I've thrown out back up on the kitchen counter waiting on a trip to the bathroom.

Well, Susan says she's with Annie and thinks that a Size 2 box should be about right 'cause it'll hold a few letters and bills and four or five catalogues. Plus, if we get more than it'll hold, they'll just rubber band up the extras and save them for us but we'll have to come over to the counter to pick them up. Harold thinks that catalogues are a big waste of trees and are stopping people from reading books like they used to. And just to be fair, Patty says that's narrow-minded thinking and how would a person keep up in the world without catalogues to let you know what's out there.

So, Susan is now off talking about a Size 3 box just so's I'll know what's possible, but you can tell she's already pretty set on me getting a Size 2 box. That's when Harold asks Susan what size box he has—I reckon they've had it so long they've forgotten the size—and Susan says hold on and she'll go check. So she heads off behind that wall that you always wonder what's going on back there—you can hear a lot of stuff but you can't see anything. Harold thinks his size box is right for us but I'm wondering how much he could know about our mail habits. By now there are at least 10 people waiting to get to the counter, but like I said before, nobody seems to care and they're just chattering away about stuff that I can't hear 'cause it's all sort of running together like static from the radio.

Here comes Susan back from behind the wall saying that Harold has a Size 2 box and that seems to settle it for everybody so I decide just to go along because by now I'm feeling real bad about that line building up and I've lost interest in what a Size 3 box will hold.

So, I'm thinking we're done, but oh no, we have to talk about how much it costs and I can tell that Susan has a bunch to say about the money part. Well, it turns out you can rent a Size 2 box for six months or a year. It's $32 if you go for six months and $60 if you go ahead and spring for a whole year. Susan is thinking that we should only get six months worth of Size 2 box because our new house will be ready by then and we can get our mail there for free. Well now she's thinking not exactly for free because she thinks we should get the mailman a nice Christmas check as a thank you for delivering the mail for free. Turns out her husband Dan also works for the post office and is a mailman and likes getting a Christmas check, which Susan also likes because she gets all his Christmas money and spends it on Christmas gifts herself.

That starts up a conversation about how much you should give the mailman in his Christmas check. And Harold pipes up and says $10. Well the lady behind Harold, whose name I come to find out is Sarah, says she gives $25 because that's what her and her neighbors agreed on as a reasonable amount and everybody wanted to keep it even so their mailman would treat them all the same in getting their mail. She thinks that Harold is shortchanging the mailman and Susan and Patty chime in their yeas to that. Susan thinks $10 is what people used to give 20 years ago and that Harold is behind the times or just cheap.

Well now the line's running around the corner out into the hall behind me, and it is sounding like one big party out there. All we were missing were the hotdogs and beer. So I jump in and tell Susan that we're out of town a lot, or at least we plan to be whenever our girls get on the stick and get us some grandchildren to go visit. So we want a PO Box all the time and will just come into town for our mail and she says okay that we should just go ahead and pay for the full year because that'd save us $4 over just paying six months at a time. Harold is talking now about his grandchildren and how one of them got a toy dog bone stuck in his throat and had to go to the Emergency Room at St. Mary's Hospital but is fine now.

So, I say let me just pay you the $60 and I'll move on so some of these other folks can get up to the counter, but Susan tells me that I now have to go over to that table behind the folks lined up and fill out an application which she hands me after she fills in the check mark for a Size 2 box and that we'll go ahead and pay for the whole year. But she says when I'm finished I don't have to wait in the line—that I should just come back up to the counter when I'm done.

So, feeling a little better about getting away from the counter so Harold can do his business, I head around the folks in line to a table where there are all kinds of forms in neat little boxes but no pen or pencil. Sarah sees that I'm looking around and asks the assembled crowd if anybody has a pen I can use. Turns out Betty who's standing in line has one that I can use.

Well, I've got the form filled out but I'm feeling bad about going up to the head of the line, figuring all those folks will either be saying, "Oh no, not him again" or thinking that I'm trying to break in line even though Susan said it's okay to do. But I looked at the line that I was partly to blame for and figured I'd be at the post office for the better part of the day if I went back to the end. So, I sorta ducked my head down and walked back up to the counter where Susan announced so everybody can hear that the next person in line will need to cool her jets while Susan finishes up with me.

Well, now I'm shoving my form and my credit card at Susan so as to hurry things along, but Susan says I should relax because she's gotta get me the keys for our PO Box and she'll be right back. So she disappears and I'm just standing there leaning on the counter with my head bent down and a dumb sorta sorry look on my face. The line is still out the door around the counter beyond where I could see to the end; there are at least 30 folks waiting now and I am feeling very conspicuous.

Susan comes back and hands me two keys saying that she'll have to charge me $1 for each key so the total will be $62 but that's only for the first year—that I won't have to pay for the keys again next year and it will be only $60 then. I thank her very much for all her help, put the keys in my pocket, gather up my credit card and a little piece of paper with out new address information on it and head for the door.

Well everybody is craning their neck to get a good look at me as I pass by. Nobody looks mad—just interested in who the new guy is. I told Annie that it was one of my goals to get to Walla Walla and get to know folks, and now a whole bunch of folks know who I am without my hardly trying, but I'm not sure that's a good thing.

Anyway, thanks for reading through my rambling if you got this far. And please send us back a letter saying how much you liked reading about our PO Box so I can show it to Annie. Tell Neil we say hi.

Best,
Sam

If a Man Would . . .

Dear Kristi:

You'll be glad to know that Annie and I have joined the Walla Walla YMCA. It's one of the kind that lets women in, too. It is the nicest exercise place I've ever belonged to. And here's the funny part—I've started going to Yoga class. Some friends of ours, Haley and Tim, who are old like us, were raving about this class one day so I figured I'd give it a go. Well, I figured the worst that could happen is that I'd provide some great amusement to the other people in the class. Now that's exactly what's happening. You know I'm about as flexible as a cast iron skillet and it really shows up in this class. One of the ladies who teaches the class tried to help me with the "down doggie" pose and we ended up in a heap on the floor with everybody laughing, including us. One of the other class people laughed so hard when I was doing the tree pose that she couldn't breathe and ended up running off to the ladies room before she peed her pants.

Anyway, I'm doing what I can to stay in shape.

I thought of you the other day and that talk we had about how Seattle people avoid giving advice to their neighbors and friends while East Coast people seem to go around looking for somebody to straighten out on how they should be living their life. Well, I'm here to tell you that Walla Walla folks have got even Seattle folks beat. Since we started living over here part-time I'm always asking folks for advice and not getting any. If I'd asked for the same advice back east, there'd have been a line of folks around the block to tell me what I should do and then, while they were there, they'd unload advice on a long list of subjects I didn't ask about, but should have.

I can't figure out exactly where the difference comes from but my friend Ed thinks that West Coast people are mostly folks who left the East Coast because they couldn't stand all the advice they were getting and moved off so they wouldn't have to listen to it anymore. That could be; I don't know. "So," he says, "they won't give you any advice around here even if you ask for it because they're afraid it'll open up a box of worms and you'll start trying to boss them on what they should be doing." "Okay," I say, "that makes as much sense as anything else I guess."

Well, I'm here to tell you that I've cracked the code and can get advice over here whenever I want it now. I learned it by listening to Austin, the guy we bought our property from. Most of the time I'd ask him what he thought of doing thus and such on The Land and he'd just shrug up his shoulders and say he didn't know. But one day he couldn't hold it in any longer and called me up on the phone. This is what he said.

"Hey Sam, I was thinking last night and I realized that if a man would take and put down thus-and-such fertilizer on that land, he'd get a good stand of grass going before the dry summer sets in too hard."

So there it was: IF A MAN WOULD. . .

I tried it out on Joe, the guy who's helping us with the farming on the land because we don't know what we're doing. "What do you think a man should do about those thistles growing on the north 40 acres?" I asked him. And he said, "You know, if a man would take his 4-wheeler and spot spray those weeds now, he could keep them from seeding out and get ahead of the game for next year."

So that's how we do it now. They'll give advice around here but only if you ask and only if they don't have to give it to you directly. They're more than happy to talk about what would be possible . . . if a man would . . .

Please write us soon and catch us up on Tim and Katy and what they're up to. And come visit when you can.

Best,
Sam

Eating

July 2004

Dear Jim:

Glad to hear that your shoulder is better. A man of your age shouldn't be riding one of those skinny-wheeled bikes. You can't balance on it. I think you should get one of those one-speed, fat tire bikes— I think you could balance better and not fall down so much. Anyway, it's worth thinking about . . . just my two cents . . .

Yes, you can get a good meal in Walla Walla. In fact, Walla Walla is a place big on eating. I was surprised myself, and since I'm like you and pretty much live for the next feeding, I was real happy to find a bunch of good and interesting places. I'll try to sort them out for you.

Breakfast

I know how much you like your breakfast. Well here's a list of places to get your breakfast with a little blurb on each one:

Merchants—This is *the* tourist destination in Walla Walla for breakfast and it's also popular with locals—loads of local color. They also serve lunch, and their bread is all baked right there so the sandwiches are real fresh and tasty. Merchants' real claim to fame is a big awning-covered porch for outside eating right on Main Street. In the summertime, it's a good place to stop for a sit and a bite to eat.

The Oasis—Not too far from The Land. This place invented the term "local color." Great breakfast alongside locals sitting at the bar having their first drink of the day—about evenly split between coffee drinkers and whiskey drinkers. Everybody at the bar knows everybody else and you can get an earful of the local gossip. Wear your baseball cap (the dirty one) or your cowboy hat (the dirty one). You won't qualify as a regular unless you go there most every morning for the next 25 years, but you'll come closer every time you go.

Coffee Connection—This is the new breakfast place in town. Just a couple blocks up Main Street from Merchants and, I think, maybe the biggest breakfast in Walla Walla. This is a good place for you because every breakfast is big enough for at least two people and I know how much you like your breakfast. So plan a short nap after you eat here. It seems to cater to locals, tourists and college students, so it's a pretty lively place.

Clarette's—Right near Whitman College, this is a great place for breakfast. It's been there forever. It seems to be a regular hangout for a lot of the folks that live in town—particularly local business folks, retirees and college professors. There seem to be regular groups in there everyday who have their usual tables—mostly men who get together to develop their social skills.

Pastime Café—This place is on West Main Street just a couple of blocks from the center of downtown. If you want a dose of '50s décor, this is the place to go—big booths and Formica tabletops, plus a big breakfast menu. Again, there are folks in town that only go to the Pastime as their breakfast place. They also serve lunch and dinner and have a big Italian food menu. I hear it's a good place to get a plate of spaghetti and meatballs. Thursday night is lasagna night—buy one, get the second meal half price.

Mr. Ed's—Way out Isaacs just before you get into the country. It used to be one of those drive-in root beer places where you ordered through an intercom from your car and the waitress brought your meal out to you. (I know you're thinking, "I wonder if they wore roller skates" because that's the first thing I wondered. I don't know whether they did or not, but I'll ask.) Those days are gone. Now the drive-in part is just for parking and you go inside to eat. This place is big with the eastside farmer community. It's a lively place where the waitresses are always bantering with the regulars and the cooks.

Tommy's—This place is way out on West Pine and the place to hang out with the westside farmers early in the morning. This is where I eat breakfast so I can meet the farmers out near where we're living. Plus it's good entertainment for them finding out what foolishness that McLeod fellow from Seattle is up to now.

This is my personal favorite because the food is good, there's plenty of it and I do meet interesting folks there who can teach me a lot if I will listen instead of running my mouth all the time.

The Longbranch—Now, if you're up for a drive, you should go down to the Longbranch in Weston, Oregon. It's about 30 minutes from Walla Walla. It is famous (well, at least Southeast Washington/Northeast Oregon famous) and definitely worth the occasional drive. This breakfast is my favorite if we're taking a trip down that way to go fishing or haul some animals. If you're going down on a weekend, call before you leave and let them know you're coming.

The Panhandler—This place is in Dayton, Washington about a 30-minute drive northeast of Walla Walla—a local hangout that offers the truly big breakfast. When I went in there one day to order the eggs/toast/bacon breakfast, they wanted to know whether I wanted three or four eggs (no, just two, thanks), three or four pieces of toast (no, just one, thanks) and six or eight pieces of bacon (no, just two, thanks). I'm afraid I was a big disappointment to that waitress.

ZeBagel—This is the place to go if Mariette is in tow. Fresh-made bagels piping hot with whatever you want on them, plus really good coffee. It's new, so I'm hoping it'll catch on. Since Annie frowns on eating the big breakfast everyday, we go there a lot just for a bagel and coffee. We can eat inside or sit on a bench out on Main Street with the dogs while folks stroll by.

Coffee Perk—It's on First Street just south of Main and just around the corner from Starbucks. A great place for coffee and where a lot of locals go to help it stay in business against Starbucks. They often have live music on weekend nights, so they're worth checking out if you're interested in a little entertainment with your coffee.

Starbucks—Right on Main Street across from Merchants. What can I say? It's Starbucks. And it's packed with customers from dawn to midnight.

Lunch

There are lots of places for lunch. Most all of the places I wrote about for breakfast also have lunch. But here are some additions:

Vintage Cellars—This place has it in all categories—nice people, comfortable, cool in summer, great outside porch where you can take the dog with you, terrific wine selection and some really good wines by the glass, and great salads and sandwiches for a light lunch. This is also a great place to go for a glass of wine and snacks before or after dinner so I'm going to put it on the Snacks list, too. Hopefully, Kelly or Jacqueline will be there because they're about half the reason for going in the first place, but don't tell Annie I said that.

Creek Town Café—A ways south on Second but worth the trip. This place is one of my favorites for lunch or dinner. It's small and lively, with great food and nice folks. The desserts are spectacular and it seems like they have about 20 different kinds any time you go. This is another place where you can sit outside in the shade and have a great meal. Marriette would love this place—lots of healthy stuff on the menu.

The Worm Ranch—They're out on Wallula Road, and have fabulous Mexican food to go. I stop here at least a couple of times each week and grab a burrito on my way out to The Land. Don't let the name put you off; it's well worth a visit.

La Hacienda—The best Mexican place in town in my opinion. The salsa is the best I've ever had and I've had a lot of salsa. The taco salad for lunch is just about perfect and goes real well with an extra-cold beer. (But I guess most things go well with an extra-cold beer.)

Dinner

Creek Town Café—I listed them under Lunch, but again, one of our favorite places for lunch or dinner. Tell Tom we sent you. Be sure to chat up the waitresses because they are all the better halves of couples that run local wineries. They can recommend some of the wines from the smaller wineries around town including their own.

26 brix—This is the new upscale place in town. It's well worth a trip. If it's just you and Mariette and you're not thinking ahead enough to make a reservation, just go in about 6:30 pm and grab two seats at the bar. Mike is the chef and he'll come out to say hello and make sure you're liking your dinner. And you will like it. Take the big wallet.

Whitehouse-Crawford—Just off Second as you come into town from the highway. The first really upscale place in town, it's been around awhile and it's terrific. Annie and I often go here and sit at the bar for dinner where you can watch them fix dinner and talk with the folks in the kitchen. Again, bring the big wallet.

Patit Creek—This eatery, once voted Eastern Washington's best French restaurant, is in Dayton, about a 30-minute drive from Walla Walla. If you like delicious and beautiful sauces on your venison, steak, chicken, or fish, this place is *the* place to go. Make a reservation. It's always packed. It's well worth the trip. Small, busy, friendly, informal with exceptional food. Hard to beat.

The Oasis—They're listed under Breakfast but I could have put them down here just as easily. If there's local color at breakfast, there's about four times more at dinner. The bar is hopping and the place is full up with folks who just want a plain old steak—big and juicy—or some fried chicken gizzards. I love this place. Loud, friendly—you'll know you've been some place different.

Snacks

This is sort of the category for things that don't fit under Breakfast, Lunch or Dinner and there are plenty of them I'm sure. These are just the ones I've found so far:

The Ice-Burg Drive-In—On Ninth Street, it's *the* place to go for milkshakes—real ones. Enough said.

Vintage Cellars—I also listed this place under lunch spots. It's my place to go for a glass of wine and maybe a little cheese. It's small, very comfortable, with a nice outside deck where you can take your dog, and the people are real nice. I love this place and Annie says ditto. This is the place to stop for a glass of wine before walking down the street for dinner. (Kelly is telling us they'll soon be serving dinner. We'll see.) We've spent a lot of good times here.

The Vineyard Wine Bar—In the Marcus Whitman Hotel, another great place to go for a nice glass of local wine and snacks before or after dinner. Very cozy. Kyle, the owner, might be around and he's an interesting guy to talk to. Real friendly place.

Taco Trucks

This is a category all by itself.

When you are driving around Walla Walla, you'll occasionally see a white truck with an open window on the side, awning out over the window, with a name painted on it. After a while you'll start hearing about the taco trucks and which one is that person's favorite—because everybody's got a favorite. Then you'll start to put things together and figure out that these trucks are in the same places every day from about noon to 8 or 9 pm. And then you'll go to one and find out that you can get two really good tacos for about $2.50. And then you'll try another and get a chicken enchilada. And then you'll try another and get a quesadilla for $2.00. And then you'll go to another one and get the Walla Walla tacos for $2.50. And then pretty soon you'll be stopping all the time and trying everything on the menu and then you'll get your favorite and you'll be able to talk to other folks in town about this important subject.

You should watch out for touting your taco truck too strongly because it's a touchy subject for a lot of folks. I like La Monarca on Rose and 11th, but don't tell other people I said that because I'll start getting a lot of calls from folks telling me I'm wrong and their truck is better. If you didn't know better you'd think everybody owned their own taco truck.

Well, maybe that's enough on eating around Walla Walla. We've only been here for a couple of months now, so I'm sure we'll find some other places for you to try and I'll pass them along.

Annie says to be sure to ask you to write so she'll get some more mail. Tell Marriette we said hello.

Best,
Sam

Digging a Hole

Here's another Larry...

Dear Larry:

I hope you and Vickie are doing well. Like I told my Seattle friend named Larry, I have been writing a lot of letters and realized that I know a lot of Larrys.

And, getting on with it, you are right. Water is a big deal over here in the dry part of Washington State.

Before you can build a house outside Walla Walla, you have to dig a well to prove to yourself and the local authorities that building the house is not a complete waste of your money or time. This I knew from my visit to the county planning department where Barry loaded me down with a dizzying number of pamphlets and forms to fill out. I vaguely remember that one pamphlet was entitled something like, "A Homeowner's Guide to Digging a Well," but, like the others, it quickly got filed in the big stack on my desk and forgotten.

Just like everything else we were doing, we were

novices at digging wells. We knew next to nothing. In fact, all we knew with any certainty was that we had to find somebody to dig a hole—probably a deep hole.

Over the next several weeks while we waited to complete our purchase of The Land, I asked too many people too many questions about wells. Here's a summary of what I learned:

When I asked about the amount of water under The Land, the consensus was that there's plenty of water down there, except in some places. My completed survey of knowledgeable local long-time residents—not one hydrologist among them—set the odds at five "probablies" and two "maybe nots." According to this survey, that gave us a 70% chance of finding drinkable water.

We did find a hydrologist who'd just moved to Southeast Washington from Kansas, who said, "I don't know. I just moved here. The hydrology maps don't help because they haven't mapped the area where you'll be living but you're probably okay."

In the end I took comfort in the fact that a farmer and his wife lived about a half mile away and didn't look too dehydrated, although I'll admit that her heavily wrinkled face and hands worried me a bit.

Jim, the well driller, said that two aquifers supply the Walla Walla River Valley—one at about 160 feet below ground and another at 500 feet. If it's there, the water in the shallow aquifer is "sweet", meaning clear and clean. "Clean" was an interesting concept, which meant low levels of bacteria that in larger numbers will shred your intestinal tract and leave you for dead.

Then he said that the water at 500 feet is okay to

drink but full of sulfur in places—so much sulfur that the water flowing from your kitchen faucet will smell like the bad gas emanating from the hind end of an old flatulent hound. (At this, Jim made a face intended to underline his unfortunate experience with such a dog.) Jim said, "You won't be happy; your wife won't be happy; nobody will be happy."

I had heard that a couple named Mae and Ray had moved from town to their new place out near us. They'd had to go deep for water. According to my source, Ray is still out there trying to make the best of a bad situation. Mae apparently wanted nothing to do with the bad situation and moved back into town and rented an apartment. I heard she's taken up with a younger guy who lives on the floor above her. The moral: Don't dig a deep well unless you want to run your wife off.

The next step was to hire a well digger and I found out that there are two types:

A "pounder" runs a well-drilling rig that carries a hammer-like gizmo and a nail-like piece. This kind of rig simply pounds its big nail into the ground until the ground at the point of the nail gives way and finally yields water.

An "air guy" runs a rig that basically pokes a big straw in the ground and blows air through it causing the earth to bubble out of the way like the froth on an iced mocha.

The first guy I talked to said, "Get a pounder, not one of them air guys."

The other guy I talked to said, "Get one of the air guys, they're faster and dig just as good a well."

In the end, Greg, who is building our new house, just hired an air guy without consulting us, thereby avoiding the need for a coin flip to figure it out. He said he'd hired an air guy "because they're better." That would have to do.

* * * * * * * * * *

Jim, the well guy, showed up on a Wednesday, just four weeks later than he'd promised. (About a week before, Greg had finally given up on making excuses for Jim or predicting when he'd really show up.) After the briefest of introductions and the required small talk about the unusually rainy weather we were having and how it had slowed everybody up, Jim finally mumbled something about problems digging a well down the road for a new winery. This sounded like the best apology we were likely to get, so we took it and asked the next question:

"So, what were the problems with the winery's well, Jim?"

"Couldn't find no water," said Jim.

So, here we stood—Greg and me—with Jim, the air guy who'd just punched a well down the road and come up dry.

The words, "Oh, shit," were forming on my lips when Jim interjected that finding water "over here" would be no problem.

"How did he know?" I wondered aloud.

"'Cause there's water over here," Jim said.

"Okay," I said. "How deep you going to have to drill?"

"Oh, about 160 feet, I'd guess," said Jim.

"How do you know that?"

"Don't for sure. Just a guess." said Jim.

"Well, we've bought this land," I said. "And we've sold our house in Seattle. So, we need a place to live. Which means you need to find water out here."

"Don't worry," says Jim. "We'll get 'er for you."

That afternoon, I drove back out to The Land to see how it was going. If we found water at 160 feet, there was a good chance that the drilling would only take one day.

"We're at 160 feet. Still gettin' 'er," said Jim.

"Any water?"

"Nope, just clay. Been in clay for the last 50 feet. Slow going."

"I thought you figured we'd get water at 160 feet."

"It was just a guess," said Jim. "We'll have to knock off for the day and get after her again tomorrow."

Wednesday night was a long one. I could hear the litanies of "we told you so" from our Seattle friends who were quite convinced that we had no idea what we were doing and that this would all be a big enough disaster that we'd be back in Seattle within a year, maybe two at the outside. I was having a hard time calculating the soon-to-be-revised value of our precious land and how much preciousness we were going to lose by proving that there was no water under our place.

On Thursday, I woke up holding my breath. Having heard nothing and knowing full well what this meant, I called Jim anyway, "just to check in."

"Still gettin' 'er," says Jim.

"How deep now?" I asked.

"Oh, 'bout 190," says Jim.

"I'll call back," I said.

Another four hours and 28 minutes passed before Jim finally called. "Got 'er," he said. "Little deeper than I thought. But we got 'er."

"Thank God," I said with great relief.

"Yep. Good well," says Jim. "Twenty gallons a minute. Much as you'll ever need. Best get out here and pick up the water samples and take them to the Health Department."

I hung up feeling the smugness of a shrewd land speculator. We had our water. We'd dodged one of the big unknowns and come up roses. I hopped in the truck and headed out to get the samples.

The County Health Department serves two masters. They notify Planning that you have water. Then they test the water to make sure you and your pets can drink it. The test takes a couple of days. According to my earlier meeting at Planning with Harry, if the tests were okay, we could start talking about a septic system on our way to getting a building permit.

Jim met me at the gate with two small bottles full of brown water.

"There she is. There's your samples," he says.

"Look like shit," I said.

"Nope," he says. "It's good water. Dirt'll settle out."

"Okay, good," I said heading back to the truck.

As I walked away, Jim added, "Don't worry if that water fails the water tests."

"What?!" I said.

"Water'll probably fail, but that's okay," he says.

"I'm sorry," I say. "Help me with this. We just dug a 160-foot well to 220 feet to get two small bottles of shit-brown liquid that'll probably fail the Health Department tests. We have to pass the tests to get to talking about a septic system on our way to getting a building permit. So, what do you mean 'we'll probably fail, but that's okay'? Failing is not okay."

"No problem," he says. "You don't have to pass. It's a new well."

Well that was about as clear to me as the liquid in the two small bottles I was holding, but what we found out was that if you fail the water tests that you're required to pass to get a building permit, you can still get a permit.

Well, since all this happened, you should know that our water samples did fail the test but we got the building permit anyway. Guess they figured when things settled out, we'd get good water and they were right. The next samples we took in checked out just fine, so we have water and Annie won't have to move into town with Mae and her new boyfriend to get away from bad smelling tap water.

Best,
Sam

Downtown

D ear Fran:

Annie tells me you're coming to visit. We can't wait! When you get your flight set just let us know and we'll be there to pick you up when you get into town.

Annie says you want to know if there are any houses or art galleries or other things of that sort to see while you're here. I'm sure she told you that there are plenty. I was going to email you a list but know you've been having some trouble with your computer so I figured I'd write instead. By the way, I think I forgot to send you a thank you note for my birthday present so I'm hoping this letter can cover that too.

So, first of all, thank you for my birthday present.

Now about the houses and such, there are more big beautiful Victorian style houses around here than I can do justice in a letter. There are so many that a couple named Penny and Bob Andres put out a three-volume set full of pictures and descriptions of them. We have the third volume so you can take a look at it yourself. Many of these old homes have been completely

restored. They face tree-lined streets shading attractive lawns. It seems like most of them have wraparound porches wide enough to host outdoor tea for a hundred.

The old streets these houses call home have wide sidewalks, so Annie could take you into town one day while you're here and you guys could take a walk to see some of them. In fact, the book we have suggests a walking/driving tour of houses in the Whitman College area and another one for South Palouse Street. After your stroll, you can stop in and have lunch on Main Street or grab a cup of coffee at one of the coffee shops. Before I forget, there's a really good chocolate shop right on Main Street where you can watch them making all manner of candies. Annie and Summer are big fans of their homemade chocolate truffles.

There are at least twenty art galleries and studios in Walla Walla, and that number probably is missing some of the newer ones. There are also five or six foundries around here producing metal art of all kinds. This place is in love with art and artists. More and more good artists seem to be moving to town— from bigger cities mostly—and, of course, there are lots of artists coming and going to check in with the foundries where their sculptures are being produced. While you're here we'll take a short drive down to Umapine (just a few miles from Detour Farm) where an old schoolhouse has been turned into a foundry. I haven't been yet myself but would like to go. Folks tell me you can just walk in and talk to the point-up artist and his helpers.

I should probably wait and surprise you with one of my creations but I'll spill the beans now: I'm taking a pottery class. Yep, the guy who struggles with stick figure art is trying to figure out whether he has a creative side. The women in my life, including your daughter, have been after me to develop my creative talents, but they're assuming that there are creative talents in here somewhere. I have my doubts, but no harm in trying. I guess we'll see.

The Farmers Market should be up and running by the time you get here. I believe the season runs from April through October. Of course you can buy local fruits and vegetables but you can also find a number of the local artists there selling their work; so we should check that out too. One of the local bakers is always there selling the best sticky buns you've ever eaten. If you get weary while wandering among the stalls you can pick up a sticky bun and a cup of coffee and recharge while you listen to live music on the market stage.

Speaking of music, I know how much you like jazz. Aside from the entertainment at the market, there's live music almost every night around here somewhere. We often go down to the Coffee Perk on Friday night for live jazz or blues. The Bistro, Merchants, and Grapefields also offer live music several nights a week. When you know what dates you'll be here, I'll check to see what's doing in town while you're here. With the symphony orchestra and three local colleges here, there's plenty of musical talent, and most of the groups we've heard since we've been here are really good.

Anyway, maybe that'll peak your interest (Annie says the word is "pique" but I'm not believing that one). I hear there's a chance that Sally and Weezie will be coming out with you and you're all more than welcome.

Love,
Sam

Let 'er Buck

September 2004

Dear Scott:

Thanks for your email message. We were real glad to hear that Liz is going to run the marathon with Summer. Now we hear that you guys are going to go watch them run. I hope you all have a great time. Sorry that I'll miss it. Right now, the plan is for Summer to run the marathon with Liz while Annie walks it. I'm sure you'll be able to get together while you're all there. We need to get you and Debbie out here to Walla Walla when the house is done. We went to the Walla Walla rodeo last night and had a big time. You'd love it. But more about that in a minute.

Since Annie is walking the marathon, she's decided that she needs a training partner. She says if we were still in Seattle, she'd have a bunch of friends who would want to train with her. But since she hasn't made a lot of new friends here yet, she thinks it is my duty as a supportive husband to train with her so she'll have somebody to talk to while she is walking. And besides, it'll be good for me, she says; maybe I'll lose a few pounds and not be so cranky. Well, what are you going to do? So I say, "Okay, I'll be your training partner," but it's clear to me now that I didn't ask enough questions up front. "Too late," Annie says, "you promised."

We are now into our third week of death marches. I am quite sure that the next 10-mile walk will kill me. We walk Tuesday, Wednesday, Thursday, Saturday and Sunday. Most days it's between six and ten miles with the "long walk" on Sundays while everybody else around here is at church. The long walks are up to 15 miles.

I have resorted to telling Annie that the Lord is not happy with us for walking when we should be in church getting a lecture about living a better life. But she's on to me and knows that I'd be avoiding the lecture and probably out fishing somewhere if we weren't walking. So we go on these unbelievably long walks at a pace that does not fit my physique. By the time we're done, I'm done in and have to spend the rest of the day in my armchair loading in replacement calories. Annie thinks I am slowly killing myself by not eating better but doesn't say much about it as long as I finish the walk with her.

So we've struck a happy balance, I think. I know the pressure for me to go to the marathon is coming, but I don't care one whit about doing it. I can hear it now. You've done all the training she'll say. Summer will be there with her friends she'll say. Now she'll be telling me that you and Debbie will be there and that it's a great opportunity to catch up with you guys. You'll be able to visit with my family she'll say. Think of how good you'll feel about yourself for setting a goal and accomplishing something, she'll say.

And I'll say but that was not the deal, so go on ahead and walk your marathon. I'm through with airplanes. I'll be right here in Walla Walla cheering you on. She'll pout for a while but she'll get over it. Thankfully some things in life are predictable.

* * * * * * * * * *

Anyway, I was going to tell you about the rodeo. On Labor Day weekend they have a big fair and rodeo here in Walla Walla, along with a parade through town. This is one lively place with all the cowboys here with their families in tow—everybody in blue jeans, boots, kerchiefs and white straw hats. There are horse trailers and RVs everywhere. People come from all over for it—Canada, Mexico, Texas, California, Georgia, Tennessee, and a bunch of other places. It's clearly a big deal. So Annie and I got tickets for Saturday night.

We went a little early with Marshall and her friend, Katherine, who were visiting for a couple of days before going off to college. That gave us time to walk through the exhibit halls. There was a whole long stretch in the big barn with one bull right after another—big guys who looked real dangerous but were as docile as old dogs with full bellies. There was a little boy sound asleep on the back of one of the Angus bulls, and several kids climbed all over the big Brahma bull next to him. Annie had to see the goats so we went to their barn and talked to all the goat ladies about their stock and all the ribbons they'd won. It was interesting to learn about the milk goats and what makes a prizewinner. It will not surprise you to know that it's all about the tits—big firm tits are the key. (Annie says they're called "teats" not "tits" and that I should get my mind out of the gutter and quit acting like a 12-year old.)

Well, by now Marshall is hungry again and says she needs an "elephant ear." Katherine wants one too. I don't even know what they are. So we find this little stand that sells nothing but these huge round flat sticky buns that are at least 12 inches in diameter. You know how I like to count things and we had plenty of time because we were numbers 33 through 36 in line. A money making machine, I'm here to tell you—take some white flour, lard, and sugar and mix it up and then fry it in lard and coat it with more sugar and hand it through the trailer window to somebody and collect $4. I'm now thinking about opening a store-front on Main Street in town. I didn't get one but there were folks everywhere hauling their elephant ears around with them.

Annie and I talked with Dave at the John Deere tent for a while and looked over some tractors like we knew what we were doing while Marshall and Katherine went to win a stuffed animal by throwing a ball at wooden milk bottles. A local group sang "Save a Horse, Ride a Cowboy" on the amphitheater stage, American flags flew from every post and pole in sight, and rides whirled and turned folks upside down along the midway—a small-town fair in full swing.

The rodeo started at 8 pm—right at dusk. The sun was going down over the horizon behind the grand-stand. Way beyond the rodeo ring, off on the horizon, was a big, panoramic view of the Blue Mountains as they literally turned bright yellow, then pink then blue before sunlight faded to dark. And then all hell broke loose—fireworks boomed overhead while a huge American flag was raised on the arena flagpole and "I'm Proud to Be an American" played on the sound system. I don't consider myself an emotional type but I'll have to say that the whole thing gave me chills. It was so nice to just stop for a few minutes and be happy about being in the good old U.S. of A. After we sang the National Anthem, the rodeo announcer asked if we were ready to "cowboy up" and "let 'er buck" and the crowd went wild.

Well, I'm telling you that the arena just filled up with young girls whirling around on horses in fancy costumes and carrying the sponsors' flags—banks, smokeless tobacco (that I think used to be called snuff), beer, jeans, and big trucks were all well represented. Then the rodeo officials toured the arena on their hay wagon. Austin, the guy we bought our land from, was one of the big officials, and waved to us as he went by. And then the rodeo cowboys all strode into the arena to wave to the crowd. Everybody stood cheering and whooping at the tops of their lungs—little kids on daddies' shoulders and grandma and grandpa whistling and dancing in their seats.

Just as fast as the arena filled, it went empty. Things got real quiet for a few seconds. Then the big screen lit up with the name Jake Smith from Oklahoma City as he rode hell-bent-for-leather into the arena chasing a calf which he roped, then dove onto from his horse, flipped onto its back and tied in 9.4 seconds. The crowd went nuts.

Things didn't slow down at all for the next two hours: Calf roping, bronc riding, steer wrestling, bull riding and barrel racing; rodeo clowns distracting the bulls and playing to the crowd; cowboys named Sam, Jasper, and Jud. Bulls named Yellowjacket, Dirty White Boy and Blender Bender.

Several local boys were among the contestants. When a guy named Buster from Walla Walla won the steer wrestling with a time of 4.8 seconds you'd have thought the grandstand was going to collapse in a heap. He made the front page of the Union-Bulletin the next day and folks around here are still talking about his go.

Only three guys broke anything and I think only one guy got stitches. A good time was had by all.

We are headed next weekend down to Pendleton to the Pendleton Round-Up. There's a two-day professional bull riding competition followed by four days of rodeo and fair. This is one of the big rodeos so it should be some fun. Folks from all over the country will be there in big numbers and the TV networks will be showing parts of it to everybody else. I can't wait to dress up like a cowboy and follow the crowd. We'll see where they take us.

So, you and Debbie need to check your calendars for next fall and mark off some time to come out here, tour some wineries, do a little fishing, eat some good food and go to the rodeo.

Best,
Sam

Wine

Dear Dave and Peter and Brad and Horst and Cliff and Jack and Bob and Bob and Craig:

It has been good to hear from you all about what you're up to. Bob, just so you'll know, I'm checking into those shotguns you recommended. I'm guessing we won't do much hunting this winter because we're trying to get the grasses and shrubs up and the game birds back on the property and that'll probably take into next year. So, you should count on coming for

some bird hunting next year.

The good news for all of you is that I have been checking into more of the small local wineries that aren't so well known yet. As I'm sure you're reading in your wine magazines, Walla Walla wines are doing real well. Apparently the "terroir" around here is really good for growing grapes, but I just learned that word and don't quite know what it means yet. My friend Tom the wine guru says that the long hot dry days here combined with cool nights are just about perfect for grape growing and the soil drains real good which is a big plus, too. The big risk is the occasional winter freeze (about every seven years most folks say) that can damage the vines and cut back on the next fall's crop. That's why some of the local wineries buy a portion of their grapes from other parts of the Columbia River Valley; it keeps the climate risk down.

Washington State wines are better than a lot of French and California wines, or so I'm told. You guys know that I'm no connoisseur but that doesn't keep me from liking the wines around here. Occasionally I hear somebody talking about some wine that's full of "hints" of some fruit or other, or has "notes" of this or that, or a "roundness" or a "fullness," or whatever. Well that's all a little too subtle for my insensitive palate, particularly since I didn't know I even had a palate until I moved over to wine country. I mostly just take a sip of some red wine and say something stupid like, "Tastes like good red wine to me. . ." I'm thinking that you guys should plan to come up here (with your wives, Annie says) so we can go take you around so you can see and taste for yourself.

The key grapes around here are sauvignon blanc, semillon and viogner for making white wines and cabernet sauvignon, merlot and syrah for making red wines. I am making a few cases of a Rhone-style blend (with the guidance of a winemaker friend) so we've got mostly syrah going into the mix plus some mourvèdre. It'll be ready to bottle in December.

There are six or seven wineries within a couple of miles of our new place and another fifty or so right around Walla Walla, so there's plenty of sampling to be done. I try to go around and visit the new ones but it's hard to keep up with them. (I know you're saying to yourself that this is some tough work and I agree with you, but I'm doing my best.)

In case you want to check into some of the local wines, here are a few of my favorites:

Woodward Canyon—They're located just up the road from our new place, and their Cabernets are exceptional—a little pricey but exceptional. Rick Small is the winemaker and he's been at it a pretty good while now, so he really knows what he's doing. He's known as one of the "original three" winemakers around the valley.

L'Ecole No. 41—Right next door to Woodward Canyon in the old school house, the wines are consistently good and, according to Annie, they have the prettiest wine labels. They've got a really nice tasting room with wine and all manner of other stuff for sale there.

Reininger—Just down the road from us. A beautiful new tasting room and winemaking building, and fabulous wines. I'm particularly fond of their syrahs.

Isenhower—This is a small winery (about 3000 cases I think) run by a husband and wife team—Denise and Brett Isenhower—who are real nice people and make really great wines. Brett's syrah is big on my list but often sold out, so get on the list for next year's bottling.

Tamarack—This is the winery of Ron Coleman who also owns the Ice-Burg Drive-In in Walla Walla where they make one of the best milkshakes you've ever had. I guess if you can make a good milkshake, you can make a good wine because his wines are fabulous and his red table wine called Firehouse Red is consistently good for everyday drinking.

Beresan—Tom Waliser, who has been managing vineyards around the valley for many years, started this winery a few years ago and is making some exceptional wines. His whole family is involved in the winery so you may see one of his kids labeling bottles or cleaning out grape bins if you go by.

Balboa—This winery is just getting started up by Tom Glase who is committed to making Walla Walla Valley varietal wines that'll retail around $15 a bottle. I'm pretty sure he's making a cabernet and a syrah. These wines will be available next fall.

Abeja—The winery is located at the Inn at Abeja, which is a really first class bed and breakfast just east of town. If you can find their viognier, buy it.

Walla Walla Vintners—These guys make some great red wines. Try their new cabernet sauvignon. If you go by, ask Gordy for his meatball recipe.

Well, that's only a few of the 50 or 60 wineries around town, but it's a start. So, I hope you buy some of these wines and like them.

Now, there's the question about when it's best to come. We'll have a couple of extra bedrooms so you're always welcome to stay with us.

One big wine weekend is Spring Release where the wineries put out their new stuff. The winemakers are generally at their wineries showing off and meeting the folks who stop by. It's a good time to come –generally the first full weekend in May if you want to check your calendar—but lots of other people are coming to town too so we'd need to plan ahead for places to eat and anything else you'd want to do.

Another big wine weekend is Holiday Barrel Tasting (the first full weekend in December) when the wineries let you sample the juice out of the barrel that they'll be bottling for release the following year. There are also new releases to sample and buy. The town really turns out for this weekend with art shows, music events and their Festival of Lights parade.

Really anytime you want to come from April through December would be fine. The weather will be good and there will be plenty of wine tasting to do. By the time you get here for a visit I should know some more and can give you some new leads. Stay in touch and let us know when you want to come out.

Best,
Sam

Late Morning at The Oasis

October 2004

Dear Don and Michael:

Well, Annie is about to do me in. She's been looking for an exercise program to replace rowing and, unfortunately, she's found it. Summer plans to run a marathon back in Virginia in November and thinks her mom should plan to run/walk it, too. She's given Annie an 8-week training program that goes from too much walking to *way* too much. And here's the bad news—I'm the training partner. Yep, they both think Annie needs a walking partner to keep her on track and since I'm about the only person she knows well enough to buttonhole around here, I've been selected. Plus, they think I could use the exercise anyway. I don't know what I'd do without all their help.

We're up to three 8-mile walks this week plus a longer walk of 16 miles. I'd say thank goodness we finished the long walk this morning, but we're now staring at even more walking next week. I'll be glad when November gets here and I can put Annie on the plane to go do her marathon. I'm planning a celebration of sitting—accompanied by a couple of glasses of wine and a large plate of something that isn't featured on any Weight Watchers program.

I don't really mind the walking when we're just walking. If we could just amble along at my natural speed, I'd actually enjoy it. We walk out near The Land where there are endless miles of narrow country roads. The wildlife is incredible. We watch hawks cruise the wheat fields. Occasionally a coyote high-tails it away from us out of the roadside brush. Pheasant sometime scare the bejeesus out of us, flushing just before we step on them. The cows and goats watch our passing with curiosity. They have this we've-never-seen-humans-just-walk-for-the-hell-of-it look on their faces. And it's a great way to meet the neighbors who stop to say hello or at least wave as they drive by on their tractors. It's very entertaining really.

But no, we can't amble. We have to speed walk because Annie wants to finish the race before they

close the marathon course, and at my pace she thinks she'd be lucky to cross the finish line "during this calendar year." Ha ha, I say.

After our long walk this morning (which took about four hours) Annie had a meeting, so she showered and ran off leaving me to develop my own plan for the day. There were several things on my list but they'd all been on there long enough that another day wasn't going to hurt a thing. So, I decided to run out to the Oasis for breakfast—a real breakfast. To my way of thinking, I'd earned it.

The Oasis is about 10 miles southeast of The Land via those back roads we've been walking. When we do our 20-miler I'm thinking we might walk from The Land to the Oasis, have breakfast and then walk back. I can hear Annie now complaining that I'm not taking her training seriously, but a training partner should be able to take a few liberties with the program.

The Oasis looks like it's more likely to fall down than stand there another day but that just sort of adds to the charm. It's a big old ramshackle wood-paneled place with a "family dining" area in the back, a "drinks with dinner" section on the other end, and a big pull-up-a-stool-and-stay-awhile bar in between where most of the crowd always seems to be. On Friday and Saturday nights you can line dance and boot scoot boogie with the rest of the packed house. Cowboys mingle with townsfolk and everybody seems to have a big old time. The place oozes local color.

By the time I got there, it was late—about 11 am—so thing were predictably slow. I took a seat at the bar. Angie poured me a hot cup of coffee (no Ecuadorian blend here). There were four of us hanging out watching the pre-NASCAR race preparations on TV. I'd met Jack and Sadie there before. They're fixtures at the bar— always there on their stools joining in on whatever conversation they can hear. They sat nursing what looked like twin bourbon highballs. I'm guessing Jack's 75 or 80 with Sadie close behind. They live just a few blocks down the road making driving a non-issue. Sadie's proud of the fact that she's never been more than about 50 miles from her home—where she was "borned" and "wheer" she'll surely die when the good Lord is ready for her. That line of thinking often sends her off on speculating about her time left with us and Jack has to interrupt her and get her back on track giving me advice about the hardships of country living. I think he thinks the advice is easier to take than the musing on death.

Their philosophy seems sound enough. You could summarize it as: "We've raised four kids and eight grandkids; we can live comfortably off of Social Security and our savings; we eat dinner at 4:30 pm, go to bed at 6:30 pm after the news and get up around 3:00 am; we eat our lunch and take a nap around 9 am and get in here for a drink around 11 am. We may be on a different schedule, but we're okay with it; we get to see the neighbors here; and we ain't hurting nobody, thank you very much."

Jack always asks about progress on our house and Sadie pipes in regularly with advice about protecting ourselves from cold winter winds, summer dust storms and regular nighttime visits from the local raccoons. "You ain't in Seattle anymore," she says, thinking that she's making a cute little joke and surveying the crowd to make sure everybody heard it. I'm sure it'll be a little tougher than we think—adjusting to country life—but it doesn't sound all that perilous.

Harold was the other bar sitter—there in his coveralls and work boots caked in dried cow dung. Harold's wife of 28 years left him a couple of weeks ago to "find something more interesting" for the rest of her life. Apparently she told Harold that she wasn't worried about her future because any future she fell into would be better than a future with him. Harold's a very sympathetic figure—nice guy, hard-working farmer who's never had or wanted much and is probably just a little clueless when it comes to the fairer sex (or at least that's what Angie says). Anyway, Harold has taken to hanging out at the bar to find some company. Says talking to his cows is getting old.

Well, Angie showed up with the big breakfast and set it in front of me just as Sadie launched into a soliloquy on the evils of a "calendar men" calendar that a bunch of local old guys did for a kids' charity down in Milton-Freewater. Apparently this calendar had just come out and was pretty much the topic of choice anywhere you went. I hadn't heard of it or seen it but it was clear that everybody else had—old guys in various states of undress smiling at the camera and now hanging on pantry walls all over the area. Sadie was just incensed that grown men would pull such a childish stunt that was bound to be a bad influence on the children even if it was making a bunch of money for a worthy cause.

Angie noticed that I was a little behind the curve and asked me if I wanted to see it since she just happened to have a copy under the counter. I said sure and that got things started. Sadie was off her stool and headed around the bar to sit next to me while I thumbed through to get a glimpse of Mr. September and Mr. October. She was ranting on about the sinfulness of it all but not letting me turn the pages until she was ready for me to. Angie was looking at the pictures upside down from her side of the bar and getting in an occasional comment about cellulite or flabby stomachs. Jack and Harold just sat where they were and mostly heckled the women about their obvious interest in the content.

My eggs were getting cold but nobody else seemed to care. Mary and Josie came into the bar about that time and grabbed stools next to Harold. These two run a plant nursery nearby. They'd seen the calendar and thought it was a hoot, saying that Mr. April was a good friend of theirs and had become a real celebrity out where they live. Said his nickname was now "Big Cheeks" and he seemed to be loving the attention.

Mary said she was an "ass woman" and hadn't found any butts among the calendar men worthy of a second look. All the ladies seemed to agree that the butt is a critical feature of any man's physique and that none of these calendar guys were very well endowed in that category.

So Jack pipes up and says that if they do it again next year, he's going to try out because he has a good butt even at his age and thinks it could really help calendar sales, and Sadie says over her dead body. So Josie says Jack should stand up and let the ladies decide if he's got any potential and he does (stand up, that is).

Now everybody's hooting at Jack and he's playing to the crowd. Angie's saying he needs to tighten up his butt cheeks and he claims he's already doing that. Then Mary says that Harold and I should go stand next to him and we'd have a contest with each of the ladies scoring us on a 1 to 10 scale to see who's got the best butt in the bar. Neither Harold nor I made a move but pretty soon the ladies are pulling us off our stools and pushing us up next to Jack who is still shaking his butt and proclaiming its beauty.

Two couples from out of town walk in right in the middle of all this and Angie rushes around to get them to a table before they end up in line with us. I can hear her telling them the story while they're walking past, and without even introducing themselves, one of the ladies says she's entering her husband in the contest and her friend does the same.

Now it's Jack, Harold, Seth, Tom and me all lined up and the ladies laughing and pointing at our butts and talking about them like they can really see them which they can't. They're talking about cheeks and roundness and tightness and size like it matters while Mary explains the scoring system and tells the other ladies that we should have our butts judged against a hypothetical perfect butt and not against each other.

In the middle of all this Barb has come out of the kitchen, seen what's going on, disappears and returns with a big wooden spoon for Mary to use as her microphone since she's quickly becoming the emcee of the contest. Mary takes the spoon and quiets the crowd saying that the contest will now begin. And then she takes us one by one and points to our butts in turn while the ladies shout out their scores and Angie writes them down. While the crowd hoots and hollers at our butts, Angie tallies the scores and gives the results to Mary who is now standing on a bar stool to announce the results. With a lot of hand waving she says she is going from worst to best just like in Miss America and that Angie should make up a crown for the winner while she announces the scores.

Well, Harold got "worst butt" with an average score of 1.3 and wandered back to his stool muttering about all the injustice that was heaping up in his life. Tom got second worst butt mostly because Josie yelled to Tom's wife just before they scored him asking if his butt was as hairy as his arms and his wife (I never got her name) allowed as how it was. That seemed to dim his chances at the crown pretty fast. He got a 1.6.

I don't know why I cared, but it seemed to me that the scores were starting out unfairly low and that these women all had in their heads a picture of some perfect butt that nobody had ever really seen. Even Harold piped up and complained that the judges were not taking their jobs seriously and that the scores were too low. He wanted a re-ride as he called it—sort of a second chance—but Mary said no, that she was in charge and she thought the judging had been generous so far.

At that, she announced that Jack had the third worst butt with a score of 2.1 and that sent him into a rant. Sadie told him he should shut up—that he'd been lucky to get a 2.1 and should just go back to his stool and not be a bad sport. So that left Seth and me.

Angie had fashioned a crown out of a shredded paper

cup with napkins tied in knots and poked through holes around the edges. (You'd've had to been there to get that picture. Not a bad job on short notice.)

Mary made Seth and me climb up on the stools next to her because she was going to announce one of us as Best Butt in The Oasis and the other as runner up. Before she broke the news she gave a little speech about the honor of being named Best Butt in The Oasis and the responsibilities of the crown, which included a daily regimen of butt exercises that would keep the winner in shape for a shot at the 2006 calendar. And she added that the runner up should do the same exercises just in case the Best Butt couldn't fulfill the requirement of the job. Angie then did a little drum roll with metal spoons on the counter and Mary announced me as runner up with a score of 3.4.

Well, that brought down the house, and everybody except Jack (who was still sulking on his stool with his head hung low over his bourbon glass) rushed to congratulate Seth, leaving me off to the side, just like it happens to the runner-up on Miss America. Angie crowned him as Mary announced his score of 3.6.

I couldn't believe it. I'd lost by two tenths of a point and could go back to my cold plate of eggs and bacon or just hang out there on the edge of the crowd around Seth. I chose to slink back to my stool and wait for the noise to die down.

Seth looked perfectly silly wearing his crown while his wife stood next to him and beamed like she'd won too.

So now Jack says that turn about is fair play and the ladies should line up and we men would judge their butts but the ladies just hooted him down saying that he was a sexist pig and should get his mind out of the gutter before he got sued for harassment.

Well, that seemed to end the festivities. Another couple strolled in for lunch and Angie ran off to help them. Barb went back to the kitchen saying that we'd messed up her schedule and now the kitchen would never catch up to the lunch crowd. Harold went back to his beer and the NASCAR racing on TV. Tom and Seth and their wives went off to their table with Seth still wearing his stupid crown. Sadie started nudging Jack off his stool telling him it was time for his nap and they needed to get on home.

Angie asked if I thought I'd be all right after coming so close to the title and I told her she was knocking down her tip with every word.

* * * * * * * * * *

Now Annie can't believe that any of this really happened. So I asked her why she thought I'd make it up and she says I'd do it to make my book more interesting because the stuff that happens in my life is not interesting enough to get a whole book out of. I guess she has a point. She says the only thing that makes her think it might've happened is that a score of 3.4 is about right for my butt. But this really happened. I swear.

So get Deb and Leslie and come on out for a visit. We'd love to see you.

Best,
Sam

Wind Power

October 2004

Dear Dad:

Thanks for your call the other day. It was good to catch up. Suffice to say that we're very happy that we've taken the road less traveled. Since we talked, I have learned something about the wind power industry around here. Last Saturday, Annie and I went to a barbeque out at Nine Mile Ranch west of Touchet where they were offering guided tours of the wind farm up on the ridge just south of The Land.

Nine Mile Ranch is a beautiful place and it would have been an interesting day even without the wind farm tours. They had a big barbeque, games for the kids, wine tasting for the adults and square dancing for everybody who was interested. Annie and I grabbed a barbeque sandwich and gulped down a beer, so we could make the next tour.

We jumped on a little tour bus and rode with a full house up to the top of the ridge. Our destination was the set of windmills you see above you as you make the left hand turn onto Route 12 after you go through

Wallula on your way over here from Seattle. Anne, who works for the power company, talked to us on the way up, while we were there, and all the way down. She was chock full of facts and was making sure we got them all. Given your interest in how wind power is working over here, I thought I'd send you this letter and pass on some of what she said.

When we got to the top of the ridge and got out of the bus to see the wind towers, we damned near got blown down. I had no idea that there was that much wind blowing around up there; you sure wouldn't know it from walking around Walla Walla; but I guess you don't put up a wind farm if you aren't pretty sure you'll have the wind you need to run them.

Once you adjust yourself to the wind, you find that you're standing on top of the world looking off about 50 miles in every direction. It is beautiful up there. Off to the east, you see the Blue Mountains and their foothills, which are a patchwork of wheat fields and vineyards. To the north, you look out across the Palouse Hills, which are farmed in wheat, alfalfa and corn as far as you can see. To the south, you look out toward Pendleton, Oregon—some of the most beautiful land you've ever laid eyes on. We could see where our land is and the Walla Walla River running through it all the way down to the Columbia River off to the west.

Turns out there are 454 wind towers on about 70 square miles running along the Horse Heaven Hills ridgeline up there. It's the largest individually owned wind-power electricity generating facility in the country. Each tower is about 160 feet high and has blades on it that are 77 feet long, so the total height of a tower is about 240 feet. These towers can produce electricity at wind speeds as low as 9 mph, reach their peak at 33 mph and shut down if the wind hits 56 mph.

When all 454 wind towers are operating, the wind farm can produce 300 megawatts of energy—enough to power 90,000 homes out this way. At least, that's the way I understood it. Pretty impressive.

While we are happy to see the area focused on sustainable energy alternatives, we also like seeing the windmills from The Land way off in the distance to the south of us. At night each tower has a light on it that seems to sparkle as the blades turn in the wind. From our front porch they look like the sparkling pinwheels we used to run around with as kids.

Folks often ask us if we get those high winds down in the valley where we'll be living. Fortunately, the answer is no. Occasionally we'll get a good blow when a storm is moving through but otherwise it's not much different from the breezes we used to get in Seattle coming off Puget Sound.

I hope that helps answer some of your questions. We'll keep you posted on our progress.

Annie says "hi" and Marshall says "ditto."

Best,
Sam

Bessie

October 2004

Dear Steve:

Annie and I enjoyed going with you and Susan to the concert the other night. I'm sorry we were late getting there and hope you did not mind having to sit way up there in the nosebleed section due to our tardiness. I think you were right that we'd have had a better view if we had stayed home and watched it on TV. We will try to do better next time.

You probably do not care, but being late to things is not all that unusual for us. We are always confused about time in our house. I like clocks set on the actual time. Annie and Marshall like theirs set anywhere from 5 to about 20 minutes ahead of the real time. They are always going and setting our kitchen clock ahead however many minutes they are feeling like that day and not telling anybody else what they've done. They claim that doing this helps them stay on schedule and not be late to things. There is no getting through to them that their system is flawed and that there is a reason for the general agreement in the world about what time it is.

I watch them all the time standing in front of that clock and subtracting time to figure out what the real time is. So why not just set it on the real time so you don't have to do the math? When I say something like that they just say, "Oh poo," and walk away.

If I am hurrying everybody up to get somewhere because we are going to be late if we don't get going, they tell me to keep my pants on and relax because the clock is 18 minutes (or 5 minutes, or 12 minutes or whatever) fast and we have plenty of time.

Well, to make matters worse, Jolie comes home from college, busts out of bed in the morning and ends up wherever she is going 18 minutes early because she didn't know that the clock was set ahead. Well there is nothing Jolie hates worse that getting up a minute ahead of when she has to, so she comes home in a huff and goes and sets the clock to the real time without telling anybody. Well then we are all 18 minutes late to things until Annie or Marshall figures it out and sets the clock back ahead.

I know what you are thinking but you are wasting your brain cells. They have been living this way for so long that that there's no changing them. We are going to our graves wondering what time it really is, but Annie and Marshall do not care. I have learned that this is not usually a battle worth fighting with them but occasionally I lose it and go off in a rant about how ridiculous their time system is. All I get back is that I am too logical and that I'm doomed to a boring life as a result.

Well enough about our bad habits. The reason I was

writing you was to tell you about this lady I met that is the spitting image of your mother. She is our next-door neighbor until we move out to The Land when our new house is done. You will have to meet her when you are here. Bessie is 89 years old and just as sharp and spry as you could imagine. She couldn't be 5 feet tall and might not weigh even 90 pounds soaking wet. Her hair has gone from gray to blue and her face is mostly wrinkles, but her mind is still racing like a performance sports car. Not much gets by her without notice and most stuff gets third-degree scrutiny.

Bessie lives all by herself. She was married for a year or so to a fellow before he went off to the Korean War and was killed. She never remarried and still has a picture of her husband on her bedside table right next to the picture of her dog Bell who is an 11-year-old lab. She's a sweet dog but not nearly as active as Bessie.

Until a few weeks ago, Bessie was working every day in the office of the Lutheran Church just down the block. She claims it's her responsibility to keep hot coffee percolating for the church members and other folks who might drop by, and keep the minister straight on his appointments. She says she also helps him come up with new ways to tell people to act right or they're going to hell. She seems to be in the middle of just about everything that goes on at that church— probably a two-edged sword as far as the minister is concerned.

When we moved over here permanently back in August, Bessie was the first person on our doorstep. I'll never forget the look on Annie's face when Bessie showed up in our living room unannounced saying,

"Welcome to Walla Walla" and shoving a big basket of Walla Walla Sweet onions and Ball jars full of onion relish into Annie's arms. Before she told us who she was, she was headed to the kitchen to find a spoon so we could sample the relish, which is her secret recipe and, according to Bessie, is a regular award winner at the Onion Festival. The relish was good and served as an unusual introduction to the next couple of hours in which Bessie pumped us for every detail of our lives and told us every detail of hers.

She claimed that taking the time to go through all of this history was a good use of time because she could now tell her lady friends at the church all about us. Then word would get around and folks would be nice to us because they'd feel like they already knew us before they met us. I'm guessing she was right about this because it is still amazing to me what people tell us about ourselves that we didn't even know.

* * * * * * * * * *

Since then we have met some of Bessie's church lady friends—Ruth, Aileen, Patty, Coleen and Elma Rose. I gather there are several more because Bessie talks all the time about where she and her lady friends are going to lunch after church in the coming week. She says that she and Coleen are the only ones in the group still driving so they have to gather up all the ladies after church and cart them off to wherever they decide to go. I think Bessie finds this a pretty frustrating experience each week because the ladies feel like they have to stick around after the service and help the minister say kind words to everybody as they leave.

Then they have to gather up and talk about where they are going to lunch. Bessie says she has already picked the place but so has every one of the other ladies, so they have to debate the merits of each restaurant before they come around to Bessie's choice because she is driving and they'll have to go where she wants anyway. Coleen doesn't seem to care where they go, so wherever Bessie decides is it.

Then they have to get everybody to the cars but before they do they have to have an argument about whether Bessie and Coleen should go get the cars and pick them up on the church steps or whether they should all walk to the cars. Bessie says she prefers to pick them up at the church steps because it takes Ruth forever to walk anywhere and Patty is prone to wandering off and forgetting where she's going.

And here's the most exasperating part—by the time they get to a restaurant, all the other churchgoing folks in town have gotten there ahead of them and they have to wait for a table. Bessie almost spits when she talks about this. It makes her hoppin' mad to stand in line at the restaurant knowing that if the ladies had just followed her lead, they could be enjoying dessert. So she spends all week trying to figure out a way to streamline the process, but it never gets streamlined.

* * * * * * * * * *

She told me one day shortly after we met her that she was all jittery and having a hard time sleeping because she'd been taking another friend, May, to her doctor appointments each week for about the last six months. When I couldn't figure out exactly how all that fit together, I asked her why that kept her from sleeping.

She said that she'd taken May to her regular appointment last Friday and sat down in the waiting room like normal. She said about an hour passed before she finally went up to the reception desk and asked the nurse lady when May would be coming out. The nurse lady apparently covered her mouth with her hand "looking like she'd swallowed a bird" according to Bessie and said she'd be back. She disappeared into the back and pretty soon the doctor showed up and informed Bessie that he was real sorry but that May had died in the examining room of what he thought was a stroke but he wasn't sure. He was sorry that, in all the commotion, they'd forgotten that Bessie was there waiting. Bessie says she said, "Oh my," and wandered back to her seat.

I asked her what she did then and she said she sat there for a good while trying to figure out what she should do and then decided that the only thing she could do was drive home.

"It was the damnedest thing," she said. "May was riding with me in the car chattering away about all her ailments and the next minute she was gone. Poof. Just like that," she snapped her fingers, "dead and gone. But hey," she said, "at this age that's what can happen."

* * * * * * * * * *

About a month ago, Bessie started "feeling poorly" as she described it. She went to her doctor who said she had to lay off coffee and salt or she was going to have a stroke herself and he didn't need anybody else dying in one of his examining rooms. Bessie says that got her attention so she has cut back on coffee and sauerkraut (which, she says, is just loaded with salt). When I asked how much "kraut" she'd been eating she said she had it on her hot dogs which she apparently eats two of everyday for lunch, thereby consuming a week's worth of salt in one meal. When I asked about the salt in hotdogs, she admitted that they too were loaded with salt but she wasn't willing to give up both hot dogs and kraut.

She allowed as how giving up coffee has been the worst part of it all. When I quizzed her on it, she said she wasn't trying to fool anybody, that she'd really just given up some of her coffee and was going to see how that worked before she went cold turkey. According to Bessie, she'd cut back to one cup when she woke up in the morning, one cup at breakfast with her scrambled eggs, bacon and prunes, one cup mid-morning, one cup at lunch with her hot dogs (without kraut), one cup after her nap, one cup at dinner and just one cup before bed. When I asked something about what decaf coffee she buys, she said, "Lord no, honey, I can't stand that decaf." "No wonder you've been feeling a little jittery," I said. She didn't seem to make the connection.

* * * * * * * * * * *

Well, two weeks ago, it happened—Bessie had her stroke at the church right after morning prayers. She fell while walking out of the sanctuary and couldn't get up or remember who she was. Coleen, who thankfully was there when it happened, managed with help from a couple of the other ladies and the janitor to get Bessie to the car and drove her to the hospital. Bessie spent a couple of days there before things stabilized and her brother got her into a local rest home.

Annie and I heard about Bessie's stroke from Coleen when she got home from the emergency room and we rushed to the hospital but they wouldn't let us see her because she was in intensive care. Bessie asked via Coleen if we could keep her dog, Bell, which was the least we could do. We were able to get Bell to spend her days with us but she insisted on spending her nights in Bessie's house where she slept by Bessie's empty bed.

When she moved to "the home" as Bessie calls it, we were among her first visitors. We've become real attached to old Bessie. She was sitting on the edge of her bed ranting and raving about needing to get back home, but her brother and the doctors were having none of it. She kept telling Annie that her 82-year-old brother, Ira, was treating her like a baby and not letting her get up for anything unless he said okay. Ira said he was treating her that way because she was acting like a baby and should just shut up her trap and rest so she'd get better. Well, this was more fuel for Bessie's fire and she told Ira that she was better and was ready to go home. It was good to see her back to her old form.

Last Friday, I went back to see Bessie at the home to give her a report on Bell and see how she was doing. She allowed as how the home really wasn't such a bad place but there wasn't anything for her to do there and she was getting bored. So I picked up the activities list on her bedside table and started to read.

"How about bingo tonight?" I said. "They're playing in the parlor after dinner."

"I'm not old enough to play bingo," she said. "That's for the old folks around here."

So I said, "Well, how about the 'senior aerobics' class this afternoon?"

"I'm not going in for exercise," she said. "I haven't exercised for 89 years and I'm not going to start hopping around in plastic pants with a bunch of old women while the geezers gawk at us."

So I changed the subject back to Bell and Bessie calmed back down.

And then yesterday she was back at our front door on Palouse Street along with Ira and Bell. Bell was as animated as Bell ever gets and the relief was mutual—Bessie was back home. I asked if she hadn't gotten out of the home a lot faster than the doctors had expected and Bessie just chuckled. Said the doctor told her she could go home if she could go to the bathroom without help. So Bessie had just gotten up off the bed and walked into the bathroom and closed the door. She says she walked around in there for a little while and then flushed the toilet and ran some water in the sink before she came out. The doctor released her right after that. "It was a stupid test," Bessie said. Ira was just shaking his head.

As Bessie headed to the door with Bell, she turned to Ira and said, "Okay, let's get on with your stupid test so I can get back to living my life and you can go back home." Then to us, "Ira's making me drive around the block to show I can still drive and then I'm free of these stupid people." Ira was just shaking his head.

Best,
Sam

Thinking

Dear Buck:

I have been thinking about your questions on how we are simplifying our lives. I will try to lay it out for you, but it is confusing to me so I don't know how well I'll do.

I was sorry to hear that your friends got separated over building a house. I hope they can get over it and patch things together. It was a good warning to Annie and me not to forget that it's just a house and not worth ruining our lives over.

I have talked it over with Annie and she doesn't think we're really running any big separation risk in building a house together since we just do it her way and don't really have any meaningful discussion about it. I think she is right, and I'm now looking for other ways this approach can make our married life better. The key seems to be not thinking too much . . . and I think I'm getting good at that.

Now I know this is way more than you wanted to hear about how we're getting along during all the changes that are going on in our new lives, but I think I should pass my knowledge along in case you ever decide to get a simpler life and have to go do it with Weezie in tow. So, here's how I figure it:

When I was a teenager, life was real simple. When I reached puberty; my penis started doing all the thinking and it only had one thought. Somewhere along the line, my dad said that I could think about sex all I wanted but that I should be nice to girls and keep it in my pants.

So, thinking was simple and life was simple. It was a good time in my life.

Now, you know what happened next, I messed up and I didn't keep it in my pants. So, life got complicated. Breaking the rules of simple living had repercussions—first came Annie, then three daughters, then all the stuff that comes with a family like a house and food, a job, carpools, soccer games, vacations to the beach, etc. Things got complicated and it was a constant worry trying to handle multiple thoughts. Now I'm not saying that I'd trade any of it. I wouldn't. But life was way more complicated and thinking was complicated, too.

Lucky for us that things were going so fast that Annie's thoughts and my thoughts didn't collide very often because we never had any time to talk. We just ran as fast as we could. We each had so many oars in the water that we were happy to have the other grab one and pull it. If she wanted to make all the decisions about something, I was happy to let it go. There wasn't any reason to waste time talking about who was going to do something, or how, or what they were going to do with it, or when.

Well, now life has thrown us a curveball. All the sudden, things have gotten less complicated. Our daughters have grown up and moved out. We are not running full tilt in too many directions any more—having simplified our lives and all. But that means that there's more time for thinking and communication. And thoughts can now collide with some regularity.

So, you ask, "How have you dealt with it?"

Well, the short answer is that I'm going back to my roots—keep it simple; don't think too much. So I figure I have to reduce my thoughts down as much as I can.

Now, building a house is a good test for me. Annie and I have plenty of time now to worry over stuff including the details of building a house. My challenge is to squeeze the house out of my thoughts and steer clear of Annie's efforts to get me involved in it.

Now, you have to give Annie some credit here. She is a skilled tester. She can be crafty and is always trying to find out what my brain is doing now that she's got some time to focus on it, so I have to be constantly on guard. She loves to talk and wants me to pour out my thoughts (unless, of course, they are different from hers).

For example, she would love to know what I'm thinking about the house. Sometimes she just up and asks something like, "How do you like the way the bathroom is laid out?"

Well, most of the time that's an easy one. It is an obvious trap. If I'm off guard and answer before my brain grabs hold of my tongue, I'll say something stupid like, "I like it fine."

Wrong answer. How stupid of me. After almost 30 years of marriage, I should be smarter.

She obviously wouldn't have asked the question if she were happy with the bathroom layout. What was I thinking? In this case, I get a quick butt in the head like, "Well, that's just what I thought you'd say. If you were thinking about the bathroom at all, you'd know that there's no way we can live with it and it's just got to be changed, blah, blah, blah." These lapses on my part make life painful. And I'm still trying to learn from the pain.

But if I'm on my game, I'll catch myself and say something like, "You know, that's a great question. I have thought a little bit about the bathroom layout, but I'm betting that you're way ahead of me. What do you think?" And then she'll smile because I have recognized her superior intellect and she can say what she thinks and I can just agree with her and life will be good.

Sometimes she's much craftier and will gradually work a conversation about the weather or something else into talking about the house and try to catch me saying something stupid like, "I'm really glad we have that great view of the river from our bedroom window." And then I'll get an earful about how we'll never be able to see anything through that window because it's too high and you can't lie in bed and look out the window and it needs to be changed and more blah, blah, blah. Ouch!

This pain has led me to the ultimate thought—which Annie calls an epiphany. I'm better off not thinking, or at least thinking very little and using my brain more to hang onto my tongue. As I said, back to my roots.

When it comes to the new house or anything else, life is much better if I just agree with whatever Annie wants to do and just trot along like an old dog happy to be along for the ride. Most of this stuff doesn't matter anyway and I'll never notice that there was another way to do it.

Annie thinks that this epiphany is a good one and proves that I can still make an occasional good decision about things.

So I just get up every morning and say over and over to myself, "She's right and even if she's not, it doesn't matter."

Annie says this is a mantra and thinks it'll be even more effective if I say it to myself all day long, not just in the morning.

I now apply this rule to everything in my life. So, I'm back where I started—focused on simple thought and minimal communication. Thinking is simple and communication is manageable. Life is good again.

Now, the next problem is that even if you master the art of not thinking and keeping your mouth shut, your wife will not believe that you are not thinking. Any little twitch of an eyebrow, curl at the corner of you mouth or hand gesture will be viewed as evidence of thinking going on in your head. If she asks you, "What are you thinking?" and you say, "nothing," she will not believe you, and even worse she will think that you are thinking something that you shouldn't be.

Well you can't be completely motionless and expressionless all the time. I've tried and I just can't do it. So, for those times that you move without thinking, you need to have some ready answers for what you are thinking, even though you are not thinking. I have found that if you say you are thinking something nice (even though you're not thinking at all) and say it like you mean it, you can dodge the question and everybody will be happy.

Here are some responses I have found useful when I get the "What are you thinking?" question:

1. "I was just thinking about when we were dating and that time we went out to the river and had a picnic and how that was the day I knew you were the love of my life and how happy you made me."

2. "I was just thinking about how great our family is and how we owe it all to you and all the hard work you put into raising our kids and how lucky I am to be with you."

3. "I was just thinking about that conversation we had about the bathroom layout in our new house and how right you were and how stupid I was. I'm sure glad you're here to get our new house built right. If we were relying on me, we'd end up with a big mess."

Anyway, I'm guessing by now you've got the idea. Don't think. When you get asked what you're thinking, make up something flattering and say it like you mean it.

Now, this is moving into the realm of extra credit, but I'm always hearing the women in my family talking about guys' eyes. They use words like "deep" and "dreamy." Annie is always talking about movie actors and how certain ones can peer into women's souls.

Apparently that is a good thing and can make women weak in the knees. So if you know how to peer into Weezie's soul, it would be good to do that while you are lying about what you are not thinking.

I've tried the peering but I can't do it. I'm assuming you have to look at your wife's eyes and not blink—otherwise it would be looking and not peering. If I look at Annie's eyes without blinking it makes her real nervous and she says I look like a zombie, not a dreamy guy who peers into souls. She says if you try to peer into a woman's soul, you can't do it. It is something you have or you don't. Well maybe you have it. If so, you should be prepared to use it.

I hope you find this helpful and not too boring. You might want to pass this letter on to your neighbor who is separated, but please scratch out the part about my penis before you do. I wouldn't want it (meaning the letter) to fall into the wrong hands.

Best,
Sam

Rhythms

Dear Mom:

Thanks for calling the other day. It's always good to hear that all's well in Nashville.

Please tell Gary we say hello. It'll be nice when we're in the new house and can get you two to come out for a visit. I'm guessing you might plan to come out for a week this next April; the cottage should be done and the weather will be pretty good.

I thought you'd be interested in hearing about the pace of life around here. You've always been a take-it-as-it-comes and if-you-don't-need-it-give-it-away kind of person. "No point in worrying over things," I've heard you say. Well, it'll probably warm your heart to hear that Annie and I are getting into your way of thinking.

The rhythms of life here are very different from what we're used to. I'm not saying that folks don't work hard. They mostly do. Farmers and winemakers alike are some of the hardest working people I've ever met. Hardly anybody around here makes enough money to hire anybody to help—whether it's moving cows or delivering wine over in Seattle. So, they're up with the sun and eating supper late. And everybody in the family—parents, live-in grandparents and kids— pitches in to make enough to get by.

No matter how hard they work, most folks don't have a lot—just food on the table, a roof overhead, some animals to care for, and a clean pair of jeans in the dresser drawer for dress up occasions. Yet they seem some of the happiest and friendliest people I've ever been around. Mostly people just have their family and their neighbors and if that's mostly what you have, that's the most important thing. It's a good lesson to us.

Another thing I've learned—if you don't have it, you don't have to take care of it. And Annie and I are full up with taking care of things. Living in this tiny little rental house while our new house gets built has taught us that we really don't need a bunch of stuff to live comfortably. And mostly we're way happier not having to take care of what we don't need. Maybe that's just part of getting older. I don't know.

Since we don't have a bunch of stuff to take care of, we get out a lot more. We walk the dogs and take time to meet new people around town and occasionally stop for a cup of coffee and a homemade bagel or a glass of wine. I'm even getting some more exercise which kind of balances off the extra bagels and wine. All this is way more fun than dusting that extra bedroom full of furniture or cleaning the toilet in the extra bathroom nobody ever uses except in the case of an emergency.

So, just like everybody else around here, we're busy and working hard in our own way. We're just spending that time in ways that are way more satisfying.

The other big change is that we're pretty much helpless when it comes to making things happen. Our new lives as novice farmers are teaching us that Mother Nature will do what she wants, when she wants. Some things are predictable—like hot dry Augusts and cold wet Februarys. But just about the time you start to count on the predictable, Mother Nature will prove out her fickleness and throw you a knuckleball that you can't hit to save your life.

We need to mow the tall grass on the front 50 acres to reduce the risk of a range fire but we can't until a certain point in the fall and we're in the middle of June just as helpless as a bug on its back. Or we're needing to plant some drought-resistant tall wheat grass in that sandy spot so we don't develop the next major dust bowl, but we have to wait 'til January when we should get some good rain, and it's the middle of June and the sand is starting to blow a little bit. Or Annie's going to need a trained-up herding dog to help out with the goats, but you can't train a dog until you have some goats and you can't get the goats until you have the trained-up dog. So you try to split the difference and get just a few goats and then a dog and then do some training and then get a few more goats—just working up slow.

I'm guessing by now you've got the point. There are things to do, but a right time to do them and this lesson mostly hits at us another way every day. You sort of want to say, "Okay, we got it." But maybe that means we don't quite have it yet—that we'll have it when it doesn't bother us anymore and we're okay with it.

Much love,
Sam

Troy

October 2004

Dear John:

Yep, the fishing around here is what I hoped for. Thanks for asking. We'll get you and Marilyn over here and out of the rat race for some fishing as soon as your guest room gets built. If Marilyn doesn't want to fish, maybe she can help Annie with her alpacas (yep, she's moved on from goats to alpacas—says they're easier to work with) and they can take some long walks in the country together. Whatever suits you . . .

So far I've fished for trout on the Wallowa River and steelhead on the Walla Walla River and Grande Ronde River. Annie was going with me last week to fish the Grande Ronde but hurt her foot while over-training to walk that marathon with Summer. I'm feeling a little sorry for her. She's not good at sitting around waiting for her foot to heal up but that's what she's having to do. But the good news is that I don't have to be her training partner any more so I've just freed up a bunch of time for fishing.

Anyway, on Monday, I left Annie with the dogs and struck out by myself for Troy, Oregon, which is this little bitty bump in the road on the way up the Grande Ronde River. The gorge that holds Troy and the river looks like a small version of the Grand Canyon. It is not an easy place to get to but once you're there you're real glad you made the trek. You stand in the middle of that river casting your fly for unseen steelhead in water that's clear as glass and cold (real cold). Basalt cliffs rise up a couple of thousand feet all around you. While I was fishing I watched mountain sheep running up and down those cliffs like they were on a playground. I've never seen that in real life. It was almost as entertaining as the fishing. There were deer, turkeys, and quail all over the place. A doe and her fawn stood about 20 feet from me on the stream bank one day and watched me fish between sips of river water.

While I was in Troy, I stayed at the Troy Oasis Resort, which is only slightly misnamed. I get the oasis part; Troy is the only little town for about 20 miles in any direction and the roads in and out are mostly gravel. So once you're there, that little town really is a sort of oasis. It's the resort part that I never found. I'm not complaining mind you, but if I'd been looking for a massage and a mud bath I'd've had to rub my back on a tree and then roll around in a bear wallow somewhere along the river.

Nope, there's no resort there but it is a charming kind of place in its own way. Well, I walked into the hotel around dusk on Monday and found this lady (whose name is Hannah I later found out) in the kitchen. She quit what she was doing to get me situated in one of the three or four cabins they have there. The main lobby doubles (actually triples) as the place to check in and the restaurant and a small store selling mostly beer and hunting and fishing licenses. There are dead animals looking down at you from every spot on the walls and after you're there awhile you find out that there's a really long story about how each one of those critters got up there. If you like places with character, this place has certainly got it.

The accommodations are pretty basic. My cabin was around behind the main building and had five single beds and one bathroom in it, a coffee pot, but no TV and the radio was broken. I think it was okay that the radio was broken because I can't imagine that you'd ever get a radio station coming into that gorge even if you turned the dial real slow all night looking for one. Basic but comfortable I guess you'd say. The bar (which I will tell you about in a minute) was about five steps from the door of my cabin—very accommodating I thought. I think it's the kind of place you'd like but Marilyn might not see the attraction. I'll have to admit that I was glad Annie hadn't made the trip; it is not her kind of place.

Well, after I got unpacked and laid out my fishing gear, I wandered back over to the main building and found the bar just behind the little store area. It was already packed with folks—mostly hunters and fishermen—swapping stories and drinking Keystone beer. Laddie was tending bar for the night and when I asked for Scotch, she invited me to come over behind the bar and look through the bottles to see if I could find some. So I did and took my seat at the bar where I was watched over by the head of a huge moose hanging on the wall beside me. Laddie set my glass full of ice on the bar in front of me and set the Scotch bottle down next to it and asked me to keep track of how much I drank so we could settle up before I went to bed. Self-service was the way almost everything worked in that place because Laddie couldn't quite manage the bar and serving dinner to folks at the same time.

So, while she was scurrying around trying to take care of everybody I managed to find a menu and sat looking through it while Tom Brokaw summed up the news of the day and wished me a good night from the only TV at the resort.

If you were a vegetarian, you'd starve to death at the Troy Oasis Resort. Meat, meat and more meat—all served with big heaping piles of French fries. You have to use a lot of ketchup if you want to get any vegetables in you. I poured myself another Scotch and struck up a conversation with Carl and Jan.

I guessed that they were probably there like I was to do some fishing but that wasn't the case. Carl works for the University of Idaho studying the health of Ponderosa pines in that part of the world. His job involves scaling these trees up to a hundred feet above the ground and clipping some little branches and dropping them down to Jan who collects them up and puts them in plastic bags so they can take them back for the scientists to analyze. I think Jan is also there to scrape Carl up off the ground and haul him to the hospital if he falls out of one of those big trees. Anyway, they were interesting people and we swapped some talk before they had to run off to dinner with some friends of theirs who were camping downriver someplace.

I scooted over to a table with Steve, Mitch, Joey and

Rhonda who, seeing that I was there by myself, invited me to join them. Well, that turned out to be a big step in the wrong direction. Steve and Mitch are fishing guides and bird hunters. On days when they don't have a dude to take fishing, they strike off into the hills to hunt quail and chukar. Rhonda is married to Steve and keeps their life straight while Steve is off "working"—at least that's what he calls it. Joey is a friend of theirs from Seattle who married a sugar momma and spends his allowance hanging out in Troy with the boys. Well, this was one lively crowd. Steve and Mitch spend the fall in Troy fishing for steelhead, the winter in Baja fishing for rooster fish, the spring on the Olympic Peninsula fishing for salmon and trout, and the summer in Alaska fishing for big rainbows and arctic char. And these guys have got stories that won't quit. We sat around laughing at their tales until my lungs hurt.

After a few more drinks (and nobody seemed to be counting except me because I'd promised Laddie I would), Rhonda announced that she was going back to their cabin to fix some dinner and wanted to know who was interested. Steve, Mitch and Joey raised their hands and Joey pushed my arm up in the air, too. Steve said they had plenty and would be happy to have me if I could walk down the road under my own power. Well, that would be a challenge, but it was the best offer I was likely to get.

Steve's cabin is down by the river and the deck out back looks upriver toward the setting sun. Geez, that is one pretty place—enough light on the river to see it moving and a faint glow of sunlight running red along the high canyon ridge.

The nights around there in October are pretty cool so we guys built a fire in the outdoor fire pit and pulled up chairs around it while Rhonda started dinner. I was sent in to get a bottle of Steve's favorite single malt Scotch and some glasses so I had to go into the kitchen to ask Rhonda where I should be looking.

Wow, what a dinner Rhonda was fixing. A big salad with her own homemade dressing, roast quail and chukar stuffed with a mushroom sage mixture, steelhead baked in a lemon parsley butter sauce and potatoes au gratin plus a wild huckleberry pie for dessert. Man, it looked good and Rhonda was more than glad to show it off. Pretty soon she kicked me out of the kitchen saying the guys would be wondering about their Scotch and that I should get out of her way so she could get on with feeding everybody.

Well, back on the deck Steve was telling another story about a woman he was guiding who went off into the woods to take a bathroom break. Of course she had to pull her chest waders down around her ankles and squat to pee. All of a sudden all hell broke loose in the bushes up behind Steve where the woman had gone for a little privacy. The lady started squealing, a fawn went scampering off into the brush scared half out of its wits, and the lady with her waders and everything else down around her ankles was doing what looked like a potato sack hop in the opposite direction. Steve said he could only watch, wondering what had happened.

When the lady stopped hopping and hooting, she realized that she was standing half naked (literally) looking at Steve and promptly went hopping back-wards back into the bushes. After some fumbling around back there, she re-emerged straightening her hair and mumbling to herself. Steve says she just walked right by him and went back to fishing.

On the way back to the truck that night at dusk, the lady allowed as how Steve was probably wondering what had happened in the bushes and that she'd only just gotten up the nerve to tell him. She went on to say that that fawn had snuck up behind her while she was doing her business and stuck its cold nose on her butt whereupon she screamed and the rest was history. Well, apparently Steve started snorting trying to hold back his laughing and then she got tickled and they both sat there and laughed until Steve says he couldn't breathe or even see very well.

I mean to tell you that between Steve and Mitch there are enough stories like that to fill up an entire evening and I can say they did a pretty good job of it. We ate our dinner under the stars in front of the fire and drank this fabulous Scotch until Rhonda announced that it was getting late and she was turning in. And she was right, it was late—almost midnight—and getting real cold. So we all hauled dirty dishes and glasses back into the kitchen and said our goodnights. I was feeing no pain and all I knew about that was that I'd get to pay for it in the morning, which I did.

Well, that's just what happened on Monday and I've been rambling on too long so I'll cut this short. The fishing was fabulous but the catching was pitiful. I didn't catch many fish but I had a great time, got to stay in a one-of-a-kind kind of place and spent a lot of my time there hanging around with real interesting folks. If you ever truly want to completely escape the real world, I think you'd really like this place. So maybe we can get over there next year for a few days. Think about it; we can talk it over at the ranch next spring.

Annie says hi to you both.

Best,
Sam

PS: Yep, I forgot one thing. On Tuesday evening while I was eating dinner in the bar and chattering with everybody about how poor the catching was, a big bull moose wandered into town just about a half block up the street from the Troy Oasis Resort. Hannah hurried into the bar and announced his arrival and we all hustled out to see him before he ran off. Well, turns out we didn't need to be in any hurry. Before I got out to the street, that big old bull had collapsed in the middle of the road. We assumed he'd been wounded by some bad-shot hunter but after some considerable examination the local constable looked up at the assembled crowd and said, "I'll be damned, the old moose just died of old age."

Well, as you can imagine there was then all kind of discussion about what to do and who to notify, but Earl (the constable) just said let's get Hannah's truck and attach a rope to him and pull him off into the woods, which I assume they did. I don't know because I had to get back to the bar where my dinner was getting cold.

S

Voting

Dear Charlie,

Yep, I did get out and vote. I know you're sorry to hear that, since I'm quite sure that we devoted a lot of time to canceling each other out. So be it. One of these days you'll see the light.

Like you, I'm used to fighting a crowd when I go in to vote. Standing in a long line at poll closing time was a way of life for me—part of being an American. Well, I'm here to tell you that I've changed my ways and improved my life considerably. Shortly after we moved to Walla Walla, I went down to the county courthouse and registered to vote. Since we are going to be living out in the county close to Lowden, I was assigned to vote at Frenchtown Hall. I didn't know where that was but I figured I'd educate myself before I went to do my civic duty. Turns out that daughter Jolie also registered to vote out there while Annie (who has always liked to be a little different) used our temporary address in Walla Walla on her registration application, which resulted in her voting at the Walla Walla fairgrounds in town.

Anyway, last Tuesday, I started driving out to Lowden to find Frenchtown Hall. The only directions anybody gave me were "Drive out to L'Ecole Winery and go to the building behind the old schoolhouse; that's Frenchtown Hall." Okay, I think, no problem, sounds simple enough. It was noontime and I was kicking myself for not going earlier or later figuring that there'd be a big crowd out there voting on their lunch hour.

Well, I turned off the highway at the winery and drove up the little road to what looked like a big storage building. There wasn't a sign saying Frenchtown Hall (or at least I didn't see one) so I wasn't sure. There were two cars in the parking lot, so I was beginning to figure that I was in the wrong place; but there was what looked like an index card taped to the door which I couldn't read from the truck. So I parked the truck and wandered up to the door where I could see that the little card said, "Vote here."

So I opened the door and walked in to a big kitchen where a woman (who introduced herself as Nyla) was preparing a salad and some turkey sandwiches. So I said, "Excuse me, I must be in the wrong place." And she said, "No, you're in the right place if you've come to vote. Walk on through the kitchen into the big hall to the voting table." Nyla also invited me to grab an apple out of the brown paper grocery bag setting on the edge of the kitchen counter. She said that Erna had brought them in fresh picked that morning for any folks who developed an appetite while voting. Well I told her that I have a well-developed appetite pretty much 24 hours a day whether there's voting involved or not, and I took a big pink lady apple from the bag saying thank you very much.

The big hall was filled up with church supper tables and those brown metal chairs. There were three ladies sitting at one of the tables that had a construction paper sign Scotch taped to it saying "Get your voting ballot here." There wasn't another soul around. So much for fighting the big crowds.

Well, I wandered up to the table and told them that I hadn't yet received my voter registration card and didn't yet have any identification showing our county address on it but that we were building a house over on Detour Road on property we bought from Patty and Austin and. . .

One of the ladies piped up and interrupted all my apologizing saying, "Are you Sam?"

"Uh, yes I am," I said. And there were handshakes all around with them introducing themselves as Nora, Judy and Peach while they explained that they already knew all about me—that I was from Seattle, and that the house looked real nice going up out there on Detour Road, and that Annie was going to raise some alpacas, and one of them lived just a half mile west of us on Detour Road, and another of them lived just beyond her, but that Peaches was the odd ball and lived a couple of miles east of where we are building—and on and on until we were thoroughly introduced, and I was thoroughly confused about their names and where they lived.

I certainly felt welcome. They couldn't have been friendlier. And in all the chatter Nora pulled out the voting list and found "Sam McLeod" on it. She also saw "Jolie McLeod" just above my name and said that that must be a misprint because they already knew that my wife's name was Annie. And then I had to explain the mix-up and that Annie was voting in town while Jolie was our daughter and would probably be out sometime that afternoon to vote.

That's when Nora piped up again and said she'd heard that Jolie was at Whitman College where her husband and son had gone, too, and what a great school it was and how much they were looking forward to meeting her. After a bunch more talk about Jolie and what she was studying at college and what she wanted to do after she graduated and whether she was married and how many grandchildren we were counting on from her, and all about Summer and Marshall and where they were and what they were doing, we finally got around to voting.

Judy handed me a ballot numbered 36, which, they told me, meant that I was the 36th person to vote out there that day. Peaches directed me to any table that looked comfortable and handed me a #2 pencil. That's it; no booth; no curtain to pull; just a brown metal chair pulled up to church supper table under the gaze of anybody who was interested. But since there wasn't anybody else there, I reckon it didn't matter. So I dutifully filled out my ballot while I ate my apple (which was delicious). After I was done I folded the ballot along the dotted line and walked it back to the main table and dropped it in the box, which was the only official looking thing in the whole place.

It won't surprise you to hear that I stood around for

a while and chatted with the ladies while I ate another apple and they ate their sandwiches and drank their iced tea. They sure were nice and it gave me a good feeling about moving to our new place. As I said my goodbyes, Nora said they were looking forward to seeing Jolie and hoped they'd meet Annie soon. I assured them that we'd stop by and say hello when we got settled in the new house.

I got back to town after running some errands and met up with Annie at the bank to sign some papers. It was about 4 pm when Jolie called and said she'd just been to vote and wanted to know what I'd told the ladies about her. She said they seemed to know more than Jolie did about what she was doing—particularly the part about marriage and the five grandkids we were counting on from her. So we laughed about that for a while (or at least I did) before I asked Jolie what number voter she was. You'll love this—she was 40th. Only three people came in to vote after I did, but before Jolie showed up. What a great place this is.

I've never looked forward to voting before but I'm hoping we need to have another election real soon now.

Anyway, I'd say that I'm sorry for canceling your vote, but I'm really not. Tell Bernard we said hello.

Best,
Sam

Progress?

Dear Wiese:

We really enjoyed hearing about your trip to Costa Rica. I think I told you that Summer is headed off to Honduras in January to teach English in a local school and spruce up her Spanish-speaking skills at the same time. I'm thinking that Annie and I may go visit her in March, but we'll have to see where we are on the new house before we set a date. Since Annie will have gotten her alpacas, I don't know whether she'll be able to go. If not, she says I should go and do some father-daughter bonding. Even if we don't do any bonding, it'd be fun to see her and what she's doing.

The house is coming along. There's visible progress every week. We're beginning to doubt that we'll be in by the end of the year however. I think Greg is doing a great job and the best he can, but he hasn't yet figured out how to make the weather do what he wants. If you pushed me and made me guess, I'd say we'll be in the house in January sometime—pretty close to on time. The barn will hopefully be finished enough that Annie can get her alpacas over here before the end of the year. So, that's what we're pushing for now. We'll just have to see what happens.

To answer your real question, I'm guessing that the guest cottage won't get done now before March or thereabouts, so we should plan for you guys to come visit in April or May just to be safe. Why don't you take a look at your calendar and let us know when might be a good time for you?

You were asking about how I'm spending my time these days. Well, this past weekend was Barrel Tasting Weekend at the wineries around here and also the weekend for the Holiday Lights Parade here in Walla Walla. The reason they call it barrel tasting is that all the wineries open a few barrels and let folks taste the wine they'll be bottling and selling next year. The parade is on Saturday night and runs all through downtown Walla Walla on streets that are decorated everywhere in sparkling white lights. All the shops and restaurants stay open late that night so folks can enjoy the parade and do some shopping at the same time. There must have been several thousand out-of-towners here for the festivities.

On Friday, Annie and I visited the new Reininger Winery out on Highway 12. It is a pretty place and well worth seeing when you come over for a visit. Jon, the architect who's been helping us a little bit with our new house, worked with the Reininger folks to design a place that's functional and attractive to visitors. You know we're no judge of wineries, but I'll have to say we were impressed and enjoyed our time there.

Afterward, we went on out to The Land and walked

around the place. Babe has really taken to sniffing out pheasant so she flushed several birds. It was right at dusk, so the deer were out feeding in the pasture. We even saw some hen turkeys run across the lower end of a neighbor's emerald-colored winter wheat field. I really enjoy being outside and seeing all that wildlife, and the Blue Mountains were something special to see with a new blanket of snow on them and the sun turning them bright pink as it was going down.

When it got too dark (and nippy) for us to walk, we drove over to Isenhower Winery and talked to Brett and Denise a little bit while we sampled some of their wine. They had the whole place open so we wandered around, ate a little too much of the food they had out, and talked to other folks who'd made the trek from as far away as California to taste their new batch of juice.

Saturday night was a real treat. Annie and I bundled up and wandered down Main Street about 6:00 pm to sample some more wine. The wine tasting rooms downtown (about 15 of them I'd guess) were open all weekend, too, and were staying open late on Saturday for the parade crowd. We took in two or three tasting rooms and, after the crowds we'd seen at the wineries, I can't say we were surprised at all the folks that'd gotten there ahead of us. We also wandered through several art galleries, most of which were serving local wines to sample while you walked around. Erin and Dillon were out doing the same so we hooked up with them for a glass of wine at Vintage Cellars and a quick warm-up before heading back out for the parade. Thank goodness we were walking; the wine had put everybody in a festive mood.

Well, the parade was the highlight of the night. We stood on Main Street with Erin, Dillon, Jon, Mary, and several other new friends of ours. Kelly and Jacqueline took a break from their wine pouring duties at the wine bar and joined us. Everybody was bundled head to toe but having a great time under the well-lit trees watching the parade.

There were elaborate floats featuring local businesses and clubs, interspersed with kids on horseback and kids on scooters—horses and scooters decorated in all manner of Christmas tinsel and battery-powered flashing Christmas tree lights. I especially liked the "Steppin' Country Walla Walla" float that featured country Christmas music and some pretty impressive line dancing by dancers dressed in their go-out-to-dinner jeans, white cowboy shirts with pearl snaps, red kerchiefs and their winter (black) cowboy hats. Annie seemed most taken with the grandma driving a horse cart pulled by a miniature horse that was wearing a Santa hat and reins of jangling bells. Norman Rockwell would have been a very happy guy out there.

Turns out that Erin and Dillon had a reservation for eight down the street at Whitehouse-Crawford, one of the really good restaurants here in town. A couple that was supposed to be at dinner had been held up in Portland and hadn't been able to get to Walla Walla for the weekend. So, talk about being at the right place at the right time, Annie and I jumped right into their spot. We all trundled down the street and settled in for more wine and one of the best meals I've ever eaten—the duck was fabulous.

Anyway, that's how we spent the weekend—Sunday

being mostly a rainy day in front of the TV watching the Seahawks lose again.

I'll write again when we know for sure when your room will be ready for you. Tell everybody in Jackson we say "hey."

Best,
Sam

Back to The Oasis

December 2004

Dear Peter,

You would have gotten a kick out of a break-fast trip I took the other day. When you and Joyce get out here, we'll go there one morning. I know how you like real, thick-sliced salty country bacon. Well this place has got it.

I've told you about our neighbors, Mary and Floyd. She's 87 and a little ball of fire. There's no dead air around Mary and there's no grass growing under her feet. Floyd is 91 and having a little trouble getting around. But, as long as you're not in a hurry and he has his cane, you can go most any place with him. He doesn't drive any more and chafes a little bit at having to wait on Mary or his daughter, also named Mary, to cart him around. Plus sometimes they're not much fun—always carrying him off to the doctor for check-ups and flu shots.

Well, Floyd loves The Oasis—that place I told you about where they serve the good bacon and the best chicken and dumplings you've ever eaten if you go in there on Sunday night for dinner. It's a little bit of a dive, but it's a dive Annie and I really enjoy. Whoever thought up the term "local color" must have been sitting at the bar in The Oasis when it dawned on him. (Annie is messing around again in my business—looking over my shoulder at this letter, and says it could have been a "her." Well, maybe so, but this is my letter . . .)

Turns out that Floyd grew up going there and knows all the old timers that frequent the place. Well, every time I see Floyd he says that some day he's going to take us over there and introduce us to the folks— many of whom have lived their whole lives out near where we're going to be living. I think he is just hoping that somebody within earshot will take the hint and go out there with him.

So, the other day as I was pulling up in front of our temporary house in town, I saw the Marys leaving to go shopping. I stopped them and said that I was getting ready to go get a late breakfast and that Annie was off at her dance group exercise class so she couldn't go. I asked if they thought Floyd would be interested in going with me. Mother Mary said, "Sure, go on in the house and ask him. "

When I got to the door, Sophie, their hyperactive black lab was barking big time, so Floyd met me there to see what all the ruckus was about.

"Hey, Floyd," I said, "how'd you like to drive out to The Oasis with me and get some breakfast?"

"Are you kidding?" he says as he hustled off to get his coat. "Holy Christmas, Sophie," he says. "I've been rescued and am going off to get breakfast at The Oasis.

Hallelujah!! The Marys were trying to get me to go out shopping with them to look at shoes; but I dodged that bullet. Ha ha," he chortled, "what a day . . ."

Well, I was chuckling. Floyd is the only person I know, other than you, who likes breakfast as much as I do and he couldn't wait to see his old buddies. He was as animated as I've ever seen him all the way out there—telling me about Mott, another old timer who's an artist and often hangs out at the Oasis bar, and Big Tom, an old friend of his who's quit truck driving because of a heart attack and now trains horses, and Old Beans who retired several years ago and is studying fiddle playing, and Mona, his wife who is often there with him and likes to hang out at the bar with the guys.

It probably won't surprise you that he told me the whole history of The Oasis and how many times it'd changed hands . . . and how big the steaks are . . . and how you can still get a fabulous Bloody Mary . . . the secret ingredient being horseradish, he thinks.

By the time we got to the restaurant, I felt like I knew all there was to know about the place. As we headed up to the door, Floyd says, "We're sitting at the bar, aren't we?" And I said, "We'll sit wherever you want, Floyd—you're the Oasis veteran; you pick us a spot."

So we pulled up at the bar and he introduced me to Bev, who was working behind the bar serving breakfast, coffee and something stronger if you were so inclined. Big Tom and Old Beans and Mona were there. Mott wasn't there yet, but Bev said he'd be along any time. There was also a fellow named Jim who is a cattle rancher out off of McDonald Road and another guy named Pappy who owns apple orchards just down the road toward Milton-Freewater. The bar TV was on and they were showing the national rodeo finals—cowgirls barrel racing and the steer wrestling—so folks were talking, but keeping one eye on the tube.

Bev poured us a cup of coffee and asked what we wanted for breakfast. Floyd wanted eggs over medium, sausage patties, hash browns, and white toast. He looked over at me and said he'd eaten white toast every day for the last 91 years and was living proof that white bread is good for you. I got scrambled eggs, that thick-sliced bacon, hash browns and wheat toast even though Floyd was disapproving. "The white toast is better," he mumbled.

As Bev set off to put in our orders, I spied a big gallon jar of Bloody Mary mix behind the bar. I said, "Hey Floyd, I think I'm going to get a glass of that spicy Bloody Mary mix; you want some? Or some tomato juice?"

So Floyd said, "Hey Bev, you serving Bloody Marys this morning?"

Big Tom yells across the bar and says, "Hey Floyd, go for it; it may be the last one you ever have." And Old Beans and Mona laughed out loud. Mona said if Tom didn't quit giving folks a hard time she was coming round the bar to pound him because Holly, Big Tom's wife, wasn't there to do it. Big Tom said, "Bring it on." And Mona said, "I'm going to tell Holly on you." And he said, "Go ahead, I'm already in the dog house—why do you think I'm hanging out at The

Oasis all day?"

Bev says Floyd is having a lucky day, because she is serving Bloody Marys. "Well, this young pup (meaning me) can have the spicy juice," says Floyd. "I'll have a Bloody Mary."

Well, you'd've thought Floyd had died and gone to heaven when Bev showed up with a big plate piled high and a Bloody Mary, and set it all in front of him. We gabbed with Tom who is probably in his 70s and had been "throwed" off one of his paints a couple of weeks ago and still was nursing sore ribs. Beans and Mona were headed off to Richland later that night to go to a bar over there where there was a good fiddle group playing. When they found out that I was from Nashville and knew what a Dobro is, we got off on a big conversation about all the fiddle groups in the area and where Annie and I should go to see them. Jim set us all straight on who was going to win the bull riding at the rodeo. And Pappy sat nursing his gin and tonic and took it all in.

We talked about the group of men that used to meet out there every Friday morning and wasn't it sad that there just weren't enough guys still living and driving to keep the group going. You could tell that Floyd and Beans really missed it. Well, it was sort of sad to think about the freedom these guys had lost and it was all too clear that those good times were not coming back.

I can't put my finger on it but for some reason I really enjoy sitting at a bar, eating a big breakfast and listening to the folks hanging out, talking about whatever comes around in the conversation.

There's a tradition at The Oasis where Bev (or whoever else is behind the bar) "rolls you for your coffee." She's got a dice tumbler and you roll five dice, seeing who gets the best roll. If you win, you get your coffee free. If she wins, you pay; but you expected to pay anyway so it's sort of a no-lose deal. Floyd and I rolled for our coffee and both lost, but hey, it was worth a shot.

So, a good time was had by all. I'm going to see if Floyd wants to set a regular date to go out to The Oasis. Bob told Floyd as we were leaving to bring the Tennessee boy back with him some time, so I guess it's okay if I show up there again.

Best,
Sam

Trailer Trash

Dear Blissie:

Well, it's finally happened. Annie moved out and took the dogs with her. She said that she was tired of waiting on the building process (even though everything is pretty much on schedule) and needed a change of scenery. I've been expecting it; she doesn't have much patience and had worked herself into a state worrying over getting on with her life. Even though I could see it coming and had plenty of time to adjust my thinking to this new state of affairs, it was still hard to get over the loneliness I felt puttering around in this little rental house every night by myself.

You may remember that we bought a 1978 Airstream travel trailer several months ago. I was driving down toward Milton-Freewater one day and saw this old trailer with a "For Sale" sign in the window.

When I was a kid, our family had one of these trailers and all seven of us would pile into it and take trips around to see the country. I have some great memories of these trips. But the one that's most interesting to me

now is a memory I have of being out fishing on a
stream all afternoon one day while the rest of the family went on a hike. I was fifteen years old. I was there
most of the time right by myself and can still remember the peace I felt out there casting for trout while the
wind blew its waves across the plains grass that surrounded me. I didn't catch any fish that day but that
place hooked me. I remember telling my Mom while
we were there that "one of these days, I'm going to
live in a place like this." Near as any of us can figure
out, we were camped on the Wallowa River at the time
which, believe it or not, is just about a two-hour drive
southeast of Walla Walla in country that looks a lot
like the Walla Walla Valley. Funny how these things
turn out isn't it?

Anyway, when I saw that trailer for sale, it triggered a nostalgia trip in my head that led me into buying it "as is, where is." I spent a few days finding a trailer hitch and getting some minor work done on the trailer itself, but, long story short, I towed it out onto The Land and parked it near where we expected to build the barn, figuring that Annie and I might want to stay out on The Land some before a house got built, and might even take a weekend trip or two to explore this part of Washington State while we were waiting on the construction.

Over the next couple of weeks, and on closer inspection, we realized that that trailer needed a good bit more work than I'd thought, but it was serviceable and things worked well enough to get by in it for a few days if comfort wasn't your main concern.

Well, there it sat waiting for us to take it on an adventure while we scurried around getting settled in Walla Walla. Many a night driving off The Land I'd notice how lonely that little trailer looked sitting out there all by itself.

So, as luck would have it, when Annie started having her little crisis about getting on with her life, that trailer started calling to her. She quickly figured that, with the barn partly finished and her alpacas waiting to be shipped out to her from western Oregon, she could start her new life without a new house to live in if we'd just move out to that little trailer and set up housekeeping. We could fix up some temporary pens for the animals and get on with being farmers.

"Whoa up there a minute," I said. That little trailer might be fine to live in for a day or two at a time but setting up housekeeping for a month or more while the new house got finished was not my idea of a good time. Plus it's darn cold around here at night (down in the 20s). We don't know how well the heater in that thing works when it's really cold outside. And the plumbing in the trailer needs work before we use it, so we'd have to go out to the builders' portable toilet at night to pee. And the stove doesn't work right now, so we'd have to eat out of the microwave. And the refrigerator was on the blink and unpredictable. It either didn't work at all or served more as a freezer than a refrigerator depending on its mood at any given time.

So, I'm guessing by now that you've got the picture—the two of us with two dogs and the two cats huddled up in that little trailer freezing to death at night, living off of microwave dinners and peeing out on the open prairie if we didn't want to walk through the coyotes to get to the honey bucket in the pitch black dark.

"It's not for me," I said. "And you'd be nuts to go live out there under those conditions when all you have to do is keep your pants on another month while Greg finishes the new house."

I might just as well have waved a big red cape in front of her face. Annie announced that I could stay in town if I wanted, but she was not so frail that she couldn't endure a little hardship for a month or so in order to get on with being a pioneer.

"So be it," I said. "You go on out there and commune with nature; I'll take care of things in town. But don't be calling me in the middle of the night complaining about the cold or the boogeyman lurking just outside the trailer." Given the look on her face, I thought—too late—that I could have left out that last part.

Anyway, my warning was just the medicine Annie needed; it spurred her into action. Annie made up her mind and stiffened her back. She started gathering up provisions and working on that Airstream like her life depended on it. Just a week before Christmas, she walked out the door of the little rental house on Palouse Street for the last time. A day later her alpacas and two new Pyrenees puppies arrived on The Land. I guess you'd say that sealed her fate. She was committed. She couldn't leave the animals out there in their makeshift pens by themselves without worrying all the time that one or more of them were being served up as coyote supper.

Now, I'm not one for saying I told you so, but I think life was a little harder out on the prairie than Annie had anticipated. You'd never know for sure because there's no way she'd admit any difficulties. But you could see hardship written into her body language.

Gradually she added more and more layers to her new farm girl shape. Two weeks into the mission, I'd drive out to The Land to check up on things only to be greeted by something that looked like the Michelin Man but sounded like Annie. She was in there somewhere.

The kids were home for the Christmas holidays. We'd take turns delivering provisions out to The Land and checking up on Mom. Jolie came back from one of her forays into the country saying that the area around the trailer was beginning to look a lot like a shanty town—temporary structures and makeshift fences around the place—orange outdoor extension chords running across the ground and into various places on the trailer. Annie was delivering a message through Jolie that she needed some extra fuses because she kept forgetting that she couldn't run the heater and the microwave at the same time.

One night when a fuse blew and she didn't have a replacement, she'd taken her sleeping bag into the framed-up new house claiming that it was warmer in there where Greg had an old furnace running to help cure the newly painted walls than it was in that tin can she was calling home.

One of Marshall's friends apparently commented that Annie was turning into "trailer trash"—a term that Marshall had never heard before. You had to admit that the friend had a point.

To make matters worse, Annie's car died from frost-bite one night and had to be towed back into town. We tried to figure out how to trade vehicles around but everybody agreed—even Annie—that it'd work better if we just ferried stuff out to The Land to support her subsistence living.

One night after we'd left her out there with her microwave Salisbury steak dinner and a chocolate bar and locked the gate down by Detour Road behind us, the girls and I headed back into town for a nice dinner out. We felt so bad for Annie that we got her favorite—spaghetti and meatballs—and a big salad to go and drove back out to deliver it. We got back to The Land and Annie's trailer about 7 pm. There she was—

completely buried under her sleeping bag and several layers of blankets, sound asleep. She was worn out from her first taste of farm life.

So, enough of this talk; suffice to say that moving into the new house was a very big day for Annie. It didn't matter that there were boxes and other stuff strewn all over the place. She had a stove-cooked meal, a glass of good wine and a newly made bed to fall into after her hot shower. She'd never looked happier.

All in all, I guess that trailer-living experience was a good one, but I doubt that Annie has been back into the trailer since she escaped it that night.

With the passage of time and the fading of bad memories, she now describes her time in the trailer as learning what pioneer life was all about and a valuable bonding experience with her new animals. She's always been pretty good at finding the good in most everything.

Tell Bahlmann we say "hi."

Best,
Sam

Do It Yourself

February 2005

Dear Watson:

Yes, you're right; it was just about a year ago that we decided to "get a life," and we're certainly deep in the process of getting a very different one—thankfully one that we really like thus far. Since we moved over here I've had plenty of time to muse on things that interest me but would probably bore most other folks to tears.

I thought it was interesting that you asked about what we're learning—not that your question is all that unusual—it just happened that I'd been musing on self-sufficiency over breakfast just before I went into town to retrieve the mail. Self-sufficiency is one of the things we're having to learn here in our new life.

Ever since we arrived in Walla Walla, we've marveled at how capable folks are and how able they are to do most everything for themselves. For the longest time, I assumed that this was a cultural thing, that the folks that first settled around here were real independent types, that the only ones who survived in this land were those who could fend for themselves, and that this ability has been passed down through the genes to the current generations. I guess it's possible that this figures in somehow.

Then I started thinking that, as wonderful as the rural life can be, agriculture is not the most lucrative of job choices. Maybe the reason some folks have to do everything for themselves is that they can't afford to pay somebody else to do some of it for them. In some cases, that's probably what's going on.

And then it occurred to me that if a fellow grew up helping out with everything and thereby learned everything, it was just natural that he'd continue doing everything and become self-sufficient just because that was the way he was brought up.

And then I started thinking that each of these ideas might tell a part of the story.

Well, I have now moved on to the next level of analysis and am beginning to think that something very different may be at play in all the self-sufficiency around here. So, please hang in there with me while I go off on what will look like a wild goose chase until you see the brilliance of my musing on the subject. (Annie says I shouldn't start bragging until I get to the end of this and see whether it makes any sense but I'm pretty confident that I'm on the edge of a breakthrough.)

Anyway, another thing we've noticed around here is that time has a different meaning to folks—especially when they're talking about when something is going to happen. We've learned that when somebody says that they'll "get 'er done," they have every intention of doing it, but *when* they'll get 'er done is anybody's guess.

In the work world I used to live in, I learned that you had better get 'er done (whatever it was) and get 'er done fast, or you were toast (so to speak). I learned to ask folks what they were going to do and when they were going to do it. If they didn't get 'er done when they said they would, you pretty much wrote them off and went looking for somebody who'd do what they said, when they said. Your livelihood depended on it. It mattered.

When we first got over here, I was sometimes a little frustrated (Annie calls that a big understatement) when folks didn't do what they said, when they said. Oh, they'd ultimately do it (whatever it was). But if they promised they'd do something "tomorrow" that could mean anywhere from a few days to several weeks if you didn't call them back and bug them about it. "Next week" means sometime in the next few weeks and the word "few" can mean more than three or four. "Next month" borders on meaning sometime this year. And "next spring" means not in your natural lifetime.

Once you break the code it's better because you can begin to get a feel for when something might happen, but anytime you think you can count on your revelation, you'll find that there are subtleties in the language of commitment that you haven't parsed just yet.

Now, you're probably asking yourself what this has to do with self-sufficiency, and maybe you're beginning to glimpse a thing that I now believe to be true: You have to be self-sufficient because you'll die a slow and frustrating death if you wait around for others to do anything for you—even if you're willing to pay. It's a survival skill.

Annie thinks that I'm just venting because I'm so anal about getting stuff done when it mostly doesn't matter when it really gets done. That could be partly right, but I'm thinking that this analysis might have some merit in the history books. All this time we've been praising the independent spirit of our forebears and their marvelous self-sufficiency when actually they were doing things for themselves because they didn't want to starve to death waiting on somebody else to get 'er done.

So now I've said my piece on the subject and I feel better. I'm guessing you don't think my thinking is really all that brilliant and I'm beginning to guess that you may be right. But it's something to muse on while you're sitting around waiting on the guy that said he'd be out to dig that hole last week but still hasn't shown up. Please tell Hermie we miss seeing you guys.

Best,
Sam

Stars

February 2005

Dear Ed:

Hope you and Char had a great trip to Italy. I'm envious.

While I'm in no hurry to get on another airplane, I'd love to go back to Florence and the little village of Montaione where Annie and I spent a week with our girls several years ago. We were there long enough to really get into that little village and the pace of their lives. Just a short train ride from Florence, we could get up late, eat a leisurely breakfast in the little family-run bakery just a half block down from the house we were staying in, and then catch the train into the heart of the city. When the tours and city bustle got on our nerves, we'd just retrace our steps back to Montaione and settle into the country for the afternoon. Leisurely walks down narrow country lanes before dinner in the little restaurant under the plane trees that became our home away from home—I'll never forget that quiet little spot where within minutes of meeting anyone, you had a new best friend. Maybe it's that same leisurely pace and friendliness that caused us to fall for Walla Walla.

Anyway, now that you're back we hope you'll come see us. I know you're a big fan of the out-of-doors. We've been having a warm spell over here. I'm sure it's unusual, but I'm not complaining; seventy-degree days in the middle of winter can renew your interest in venturing out.

While you guys were seeing the world, Annie and I moved into the new house. There are still a bunch of boxes stacked up out on the porch waiting to be unpacked, but we're in no hurry to tackle them. For the first time in our lives, we're just taking our time and breaking open a new box when the mood strikes us.

Yesterday afternoon, Annie and I took the dogs on a long walk down along the river where we collected some kindling and a few logs for a fire. We also checked up on the spring that feeds the shallow ponds just below the house. The ducks and geese love those ponds because they're full of grass and the insects they feed on. We get real pleasure out of watching their acrobatics as they fly in and away. Since we moved the cattle off the place, we've noticed that the pheasants and turkeys are starting to come back. The dogs think they have a shot at catching the pheasant we flush while wandering along the edge of the ponds, but I doubt we're any real threat to the bird life around here.

We got back to the house about sunset—just in time to watch the setting sun turn the wispy clouds hanging out over the Blue Mountains from bright pink to deep purple. The air was cooling off but still warm enough to be outside with a light sweater on. Annie said she'd set our inaugural fire in the outdoor fireplace if I'd open a bottle of wine and find her a blanket. Sounded like a deal to me.

Once we got our fire roaring, we pulled a couple of rocking chairs up close and settled in to watch the flames blacken the virgin brick lining the firebox. Annie just snuggled into her blanket and dozed off between sips of wine while I entertained the dogs huddled up around my rocker.

One thing we've learned already—when it gets dark in the country, it gets real dark. Aside from the lights on inside the house, there's almost no man-made light polluting the night sky.

While Annie snoozed in front of the fire on the porch, I went inside and turned off all the lights. Well, I may as well have been in the haunted house at the fair. I couldn't see a thing as I stumbled my way back out onto the porch. There you could see within the limits of the firelight, but no further.

I stepped out to the edge of the porch, looked up into the moonless sky and remembered why we were here on The Land. I've never seen stars like that. The sky was full up with the Milky Way, Orion's Belt, Cassiopeia and the Big Dipper—all blazing out of the southern sky. A satellite sailed across the sky faster than I remember ever seeing.

There were a few farm lights on at the Bertrand's place down the road, but those were the only neighbor's lights I could see.

I woke Annie up and listened to her slurred tale about how she wasn't really sleeping before I managed to get her out of her rocker to see the sky. I knew she'd be awestruck but never would have predicted that she'd grab up her blanket to lead me out into the pasture in front of the house to lie in the grass and watch the sky go by. I guess I'd begun to think I was a little too old for that foolishness.

I haven't done that since college days and I was surprised to find that lying with your back pressed against the cool earth while gazing at a moonless sky full of stars is just as exciting as it was back in the good ole days. We lay there all bundled up in that blanket and watched the sky move slowly by. Aside from the occasional "wow" or reprimand directed at one of the dogs, we didn't say a word. I guess there was nothing to say.

Lying there seemed to have waked up something in both of us that reconnected us with the universe; it was pretty humbling. It always makes me feel insignificant.

For the longest time neither of us moved, and the dogs settled in very still around us. The stars blinked away at us, delivering the light that had left them to find its way into our eyes millions of years later. Who'd've thought that we'd be there to receive it.

After awhile the cold night got to Annie, and my stomach started grumbling—ordinary stuff working its way back into our brains. We needed to get back inside and fix some supper, but before we got up Annie grabbed my hand and said, "Welcome to Walla Walla."

"I'm glad to be here," I said.

"So am I," she said.

Best,
Sam